Global Stage

Language Book 2

Roisin O'Farrell and Jeanette Corbett

CB127281

macmillan education

Scope and Sequence

Unit	Vocabulary	Explore Language	Global Citizenship
Language Review	**Vocabulary** *Animals, Activities, Clothes, Family, Food, Home, Places in a Town* **Grammar** *Question Words, Possessive Adjectives and Pronouns, There Is/Are, Present Progressive, Simple Present*		
1 What Does It Do? page 10	**Gadgets** *alarm clock, cell phone, computer, keyboard, laptop, mouse, radio, screen, tablet, TV, video game* **Places and Objects in School** *bookcase, cafeteria, classroom, gym, hallway, language lab, playground, projector, whiteboard* **Song** *Living in a Modern World*	Simple Present: Adverbs of Frequency *How often …?* *always / often / sometimes / rarely / never* Present Progressive Review	How is technology in schools different around the world? **Listening Skills** Listening for gist and details.
2 Thank You page 22	**Food** *cherry, chicken, corn, cupcake, eggplant, fruit, peas, pineapple, rice, sausage, spinach, tomato* **Containers, Food and Drink** *a bag of, a bottle of, a bowl of, a box of, a can of, a carton of, lemonade, potato chips, soup* **Song** *It's Market Day!*	Quantifiers: *a lot of, much, many* Quantifiers with questions: *How much …? How many …? Some / Any*	How is fruit different around the world? **Listening Skills** Listening for gist and details.
Put It Together	**Review Units 1 and 2** *Lemonade for Everyone*		
3 It Keeps Changing page 36	**Nature** *beach, desert, forest, glacier, island, lake, ocean, mountain, river, valley, waterfall* **Animals** *bear, chameleon, duck, feathers, fur, penguin, scales, snake, swan* **Song** *It's a Wonderful World*	Simple Past: *be* statements Simple Past: *be* questions	How do animals change? **Listening Skills** Listening for gist and details.
4 What Happened? page 48	**Action Verbs 1** *bake, carry, clap, compete, dance, drop, start, study, trip* **Action Verbs 2** *bounce, finish, learn, move, pack, play, practice, smile, travel, wait* **Song** *It's OK*	Simple Past: Regular verb statements Simple Past: Regular verb questions	What is special about a first day at school? **Listening Skills** Listening for gist and details.
Put It Together	**Review Units 3 and 4** *Explore the Island*		
5 Let's Go Back page 62	**Parts of the Body and Adjectives** *body, claws, dangerous, dinosaur, huge, scary, slow, tail, tiny, wings* **Fossils and Ruins** *bones, broken, build, dig, find, fossil, jug, pottery, skeleton* **Song** *King of the Dinosaurs*	Simple Past: Irregular verb statements Simple Past: Irregular verb questions	Where can we learn about the past in different countries? **Listening Skills** Listening for gist and details.

Speaking	Writing	International English	Literacy Book
Presentation Describing Technology **Pronunciation** /eɪ/ and /e/	**Punctuation** Periods and question marks **Product** A Technology Survey	**US** *cell phone; rarely; hallway* **UK** *mobile phone; hardly ever; corridor*	**Story** *The After-School Inventor* **Instructional Text** *My Good Ideas Book* **Reading Skill** Identifying a Sequence of Events
Conversation Making Suggestions, Discussing Needs **Pronunciation** /l/ and /r/	**Punctuation** Capital letters and commas **Product** A Description of My Kitchen	**US** *eggplant; cupcake; potato chips* **UK** *aubergine; fairy cake; crisps*	**Informational Text** *Chuseok: Korea's Harvest Festival* **Science Fiction** *First Harvest* **Reading Skill** Understanding the Setting
Conversation Showing Enthusiasm **Pronunciation** /ɑr/ and /ʌ/	**Sentence Building** *and, but* **Product** A Postcard		**Poem** *The Bear and I* **Informational Text** *Clean Cars* **Reading Skill** Comparing and Contrasting Information
Presentation Describing an Important Event **Pronunciation** /d/ and /t/ or /ɪd/	**Spelling** Regular verb endings **Product** A Description of an Event	**US** *practice* **UK** *practise*	**Informational Text** *Where Is She?* **Story** *The Angry Mountain* **Reading Skill** Identifying Cause and Effect
Presentation Describing a Dinosaur **Pronunciation** /oʊ/ and /ɔr/	**Sentence Building** *because* **Product** A Diary		**Fantasy** *The Time Book* **Informational Text** *Time Capsules* **Reading Skill** Identifying the Main Idea and Details

Unit	Vocabulary	Explore Language	Global Citizenship
6 Look What I Made page 74	**Art and Physical Characteristics** *beard, box, curly, drawing, jewelry, mask, mustache, painting, sculpture, straight* **Short Adjectives** *building, clean, hard, messy, new, noisy, quiet, soft, thick, wall* **Song** *Get Creative*	Comparatives: Short Adjectives Superlatives: Short Adjectives	Which famous places in the world are amazing? **Listening Skills** Listening for gist and details.
Put It Together	**Review Units 5 and 6** *Race to the Museum*		
7 We're a Team page 88	**Activities** *acting, biking, climbing, horseback riding, kayaking, sailing, skating, singing, waterskiing, windsurfing, yoga* **Working with Others** *borrow, club, community, give, help each other, share, take turns, trade, work together* **Song** *Teamwork Is Number One*	Telling the Time Modal Verbs: *can* for permission, requests, and offers	How do people work as a team in different communities? **Listening Skills** Listening for gist and details.
8 You're My Hero page 100	**Sports and Long Adjectives** *difficult, exciting, gymnastics, patient, popular, race, strong, tennis, track and field, volleyball* **Attributes** *beautiful, brave, friendly, helpful, intelligent, interesting, mean, selfish, thoughtful* **Song** *Who's Your Hero?*	Comparatives: Long Adjectives Superlatives: Long Adjectives	Who are heroes around the world? **Listening Skills** Listening for gist and details.
Put It Together	**Review Units 7 and 8** *Give Me a Clue*		
9 Do You Live Here? page 114	**Around the Home** *attic, balcony, basement, bathtub, cabinet, castle, closet, fridge, lamp, stairs, stove, tower* **Emotions** *angry, annoyed, bored, excited, frightened, happy, proud, sad, surprised, tired* **Song** *In the Scary Castle*	Simple Past: regular and irregular verbs *There Was / There Were*	Why do people visit castles? **Listening Skills** Listening for gist and details.
10 Are We There Yet? page 126	**Journeys** *airport, boat, country, journey, passport, plane, station, suitcase, ticket, traffic* **Weather** *cloudy, foggy, lightning, rain, rainbow, snow, storm, sunny, thunder, windy* **Song** *Let's Go on a Journey*	Future Plans: *going to* statements Prepositions of Movement *through / around / up / down / under / over*	How does weather change journeys to school around the world? **Listening Skills** Listening for gist and details.
Put It Together	**Review Units 9 and 10** *Day by Day: Find the Differences*		
Plays page 140	Play 1 *Adventures on Purple Mountain* (Units 1–5) Play 2 *King Grandpa's Treasure* (Units 6–10)		

Speaking	Writing	International English	Literacy Book
Presentation Giving Instructions **Pronunciation** /g/ and /k/	**Spelling** Comparative and superlative endings **Product** A Personal Profile	**US** *jewelry; mustache; clean* **UK** *jewellery; moustache; tidy*	**Story** *The Superstar* **Informational Text** *Visit Gaudí's World* **Reading Skill** Identifying Fact and Opinion
Conversation Deciding What to Do **Pronunciation** /n/ and /ŋ/	**Sentence Building** Imperatives **Product** Team Game Instructions	**US** *horseback riding, biking; trade* **UK** *horse-riding, cycling; swap*	**Informational Text** *Great Teamwork* **Story** *It's Mine* **Reading Skill** Predicting Endings
Conversation Taking Turns and Playing Games **Pronunciation** /oʊ/ and /aʊ/	**Sentence Building** *I think, because* **Product** A Hero Profile	**US** *track and field; math* **UK** *athletics; maths*	**Biography** *In First Place* **Play** *A New Hero* **Reading Skill** Understanding Characters
Presentation Describing Your Dream House **Pronunciation** /s/ and /ð/	**Sentence Building** Sequencers **Product** A Picture Story	**US** *stove, bathtub* **UK** *cooker, bath*	**Fable** *The Clever King* **Informational Text** *Amazing Castles* **Reading Skill** Scanning for Specific Information
Conversation Buying a Ticket **Pronunciation** /r/ and /w/	**Text Type** Emails **Product** An Amazing Journey Email	**US** *country; round-trip* **UK** *countryside; return*	**Story** *Young Nicholas* **Biography** *The Thirty-Year Journey* **Reading Skill** Identifying the Sequence of Events

A Listen and number. Who's Frank?

B Look and write. What can you see?

Animals	Food
frog	carrots

C Look, unscramble, and write.

1  chtaw VT watch TV

2 

eadr micoc ksoob ____________

3  od lletab ____________

4  naitp a cipreut ____________

5  keam ocokesi ____________

6  aply osccre ____________

7  og rfunisg ____________

8  og wsmingim ____________

D Think and write.

Across

3 You can do sports here.
5 You play outside here.
6 You can make cookies here.
8 You sleep here on vacation.

Down

1 Doctors work here.
2 You go to bed here.
4 You brush your teeth here.
7 You can eat here.

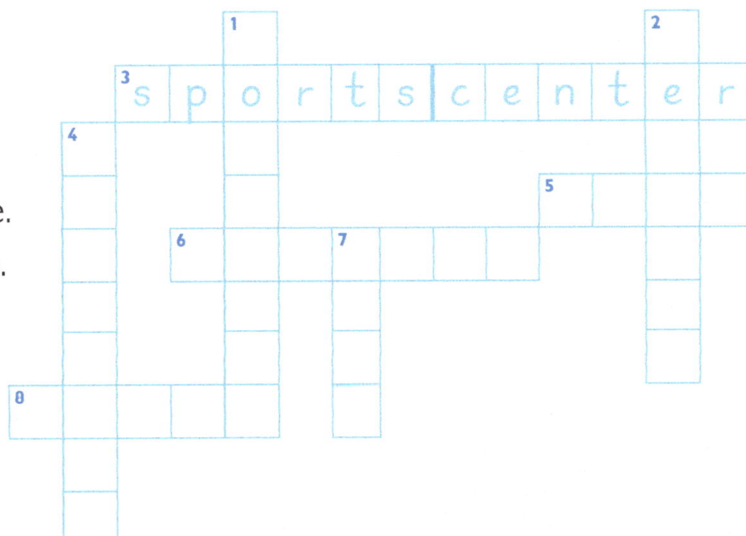

A Listen and choose.

B Read and match.

1 Grandma has a hat with a flower.
2 Sam has a red hat.
3 That's not your food.
4 These aren't our spoons.

a. It's theirs.
b. That's his hat.
c. That's her hat.
d. They're yours.

C Look at A. Read and choose.

1 The twins are / aren't sleeping.
2 Sam is / isn't wearing a gray T-shirt.
3 The children are sitting / sit on the grass.
4 One penguin aren't / isn't wearing a hat.
5 The crocodile is / are swimming in the lake.

D **Look at A. Read and complete with *is*, *isn't*, *are*, or *aren't*.**

1 There __isn't__ any soup.
2 There ______ any hippos.
3 There ______ five flowers.
4 There ______ a café.
5 There ______ a lake.

E **Read and complete. Then match.**

has	~~'m~~	can	eat	're

1 I can swim. I __'m__ gray.
2 They ______ black and white.
They ______ run.
3 He ______ a big mouth and teeth.
He doesn't ______ leaves.

a. He's a tiger.
b. I'm a hippo.
c. They're zebras.

UNIT 1

What Does It Do?

A Listen and find. Where's Luke?

B Listen, say, and number the pictures in A.

C Listen. Close your eyes and visualize.

D **Look and write.**

Has a screen	Doesn't have a screen
cell phone	keyboard

E **Listen and sing. Then watch and sing.**

Living in a Modern World

Living in a modern world,
With a lot of cool technology.
Living in a digital world.
It's so easy for you and me.

With my computer, yeah, yeah,
I can learn about the world.
And for music, yeah, yeah,
I can listen to the radio.

I use my tablet, yeah, yeah,
To watch movies and play games, too.
And when I'm lonely, yeah, yeah,
I use a cell phone to talk to you.

A Listen and read. Who does Grandpa email?

B Look at A. Complete.

Adverbs of Frequency

How often	______	you	______	this tablet?
	does	he		

We	sometimes watch	movies.	I	______	use	the computer.

Remember

I use a laptop.
But She uses a laptop.

C Think and discuss. Then choose and complete.

1 We use adverbs of frequency to say how many times / when we do something.

2 never ______ ______ often always

D Listen and say.

E Put the words in order.

1 watches / dad / My / never / TV.
My dad never watches TV.

2 I / video games / on a tablet. / rarely / play
______

3 the radio. / My grandparents / often / listen to
______

4 sometimes / I / watch / on my dad's laptop. / movies
______

F Write questions about your friends. Then ask and answer.

How often does Ali watch TV?
How often does Sue ...?
______

How often do you watch TV, Ali?

I rarely watch TV.

How is technology in schools different around the world?

A Listen to Teddy talk to Olivia about his school. Does Teddy's school have technology?

bookcase ☐

language lab ☐

projector ☐

cafeteria ☐

hallway ☐

hallway (US) / corridor (UK)

gym ☐

whiteboard 1

classroom ☐

playground ☐

B Listen, say, and number the pictures in A.

C Play *Word Tennis* with a friend.

D Now listen to Olivia and Akash. Number the pictures. Who uses technology at school?

a

Olivia, UK ☐

b

Akash, Bangladesh ☐

E Listen again. Write *True* or *False*.

1 Akash has his lessons on a screen. True

2 His teacher is in a different place. ______

3 He can't speak to his teacher. ______

4 Olivia doesn't have a computer at school. ______

5 She doesn't have fun at her school. ______

**What technology do you like using?
Do people need technology to learn? Why?**

A Listen and read. Who sends Dad a message?

B Look at A. Complete.

Present Progressive Review

I	______	talking	to Luis.	They	aren't	watching	movies.
He	______	send____	messages.	She	isn't	talking	to Dad.
______	you	talking	to me?	No, ______ .		Yes, I am.	

Remember
use → using

C Think and discuss. Then choose.

1 We use the present progressive to talk about actions happening now / in the past.

D Listen and say.

E Read and complete in present progressive.

Hi Mom!

I'm at school. 1 I 'm writing (write) a message on the computer. I can see Cousin Paula on the playground with her friends. 2 They ______ (play) basketball. Oh, no! 3 Paula ______ (not listen) to the teacher! 4 ______ you ______ (use) your tablet?

See you later!

F Play a guessing game. Mime. Then ask and answer.

laptop tablet playground gym cafeteria video game radio language lab

Are you running on the playground?

No, I'm not. I'm running in the gym.

Take the Stage

A Watch and listen. Why is a laptop useful?

B Watch again. Check (✓) the phrases you hear.

1 ✓ Hello, my name's Grace.
2 ◯ My presentation is about laptops.
3 ◯ You can use a laptop to find information.
4 ◯ I often go online.
5 ◯ You can also use a laptop to plan a presentation.
6 ◯ I sometimes use books from the library instead.
7 ◯ A laptop is great for pictures.
8 ◯ A cell phone is useful because it has a screen and a keyboard.
9 ◯ Thank you.

Pronunciation /eɪ/ and /e/

Listen and say.

name Grace great help instead when

What other words do you know with these sounds?

C Plan. Think about the technology you like. Choose (✓) two and complete.

◯ computer ◯ radio ◯ TV ◯ laptop
◯ cell phone ◯ tablet

Technology	It has/doesn't have …	You can/can't …	I …
laptop	a screen	find information	draw pictures

D Prepare your presentation. Use your ideas from C and phrases from B.

Introduce your presentation Hello, my name's ... ____________

____

Talk about the technology you like ____________

____

____

____

____

Finish ____________

E Practice with a friend. Then share with your class.

Reflect
Did I speak clearly?
Yes / No

Write About It

A Read the survey and answers. Underline the question marks (?) and circle the periods (.).

Let's Talk Technology!

• What technology do you use? • How often do you use it? • What's your favorite technology? • Is your teacher using technology today?	I use a tablet and a TV. I often watch the TV and I sometimes use the tablet. My favorite technology is my tablet. I use it to play games. Today, my teacher isn't using her cell phone. She's using a laptop. We use technology a lot!

When do we use question marks?

B Write the question marks and periods.

1 My school has a cafeteria.

2 Do you use a laptop

3 How often does your dad use his cell phone

4 My grandma has a computer

5 Are you doing your homework

C Plan. Think about the survey questions. Complete.

1 What technology do you use? tablet, ______

2 How often do you use it? sometimes, ______

3 What's your favorite technology? ______

4 Is your teacher using technology today? ______

D Write your answers to the survey.

Reflect
Did I use periods?

Read the questions and draw or write your answers.

What did I do?

What did I learn?

How did I learn?

How well did I do?

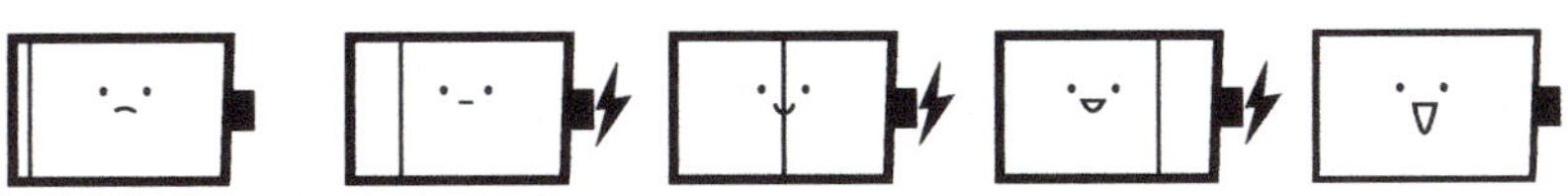

What can I do next?

- Read
- Sing
- Play
- Talk

UNIT 2

Thank You

A Listen and find. What's Lucy making?

B Listen, say, and number the pictures in **A**.

C Listen. Close your eyes and visualize.

1 trifu fruit
2 sape ______
3 reci ______
4 taglepgn ______
5 gasuase ______
6 chipans ______
7 mottao ______
8 norc ______
9 palpenipe ______
10 packuce ______
11 nechick ______
12 ryhcer ______

eggplant cupcake
aubergine fairy cake

D **Look, unscramble, and write.**

E **Listen and sing. Then watch and sing.**

It's Market Day!

It's market day! Hooray! Hooray!
It's market day today!

There are tomatoes and peas.
Some spinach? Yes, please!
Look! Cupcakes with cherries on top!

There's chicken and rice.
Those sausages look nice!
And cupcakes with cherries on top!

There are eggplants and corn.
Pineapples and more!
And yes! Cupcakes with cherries on top!

Explore Language

A Listen and read. What fruit does Mr. Bell have?

1

B Look at **A**. Complete.

A Lot of, Much, Many

Count Nouns				Noncount Nouns			
You	don't have	______	cherries.	I	don't have	______	fruit.
You	have	a lot of	pineapples.	We	need	______	fruit.

You can't count noncount nouns.
Remember

C Think and discuss. Then choose.

1 We use *a lot of* to talk about
large quantities / small quantities.

2 We use *not many* and *not much* to talk about
large quantities / small quantities.

D Listen and say.

E Read and complete with *a lot of*, *much*, or *many*.

Ling: I want to make lunch for Mom and Dad.
I have **1** a lot of chicken.

Mr. Bell: OK. Do you have vegetables?

Ling: No, I don't have **2** ______ vegetables. I need
3 ______ peas.

Mr. Bell: Chicken, peas … Do you need any fruit?

Ling: I don't have **4** ______ fruit. But I have
5 ______ cupcakes!

F Play a game. Draw your lunch. Then guess.

Guess my lunch.

You don't have many peas.

No! I have a lot of peas!

pineapple sausage cupcake peas
rice eggplant cherry tomato

How is fruit different around the world?

A Listen to Basilio talk to his mom about lunch. What does he have in his lunchbox?

a bottle of ☐

a can of ☐

a box of 1

a carton of ☐

a bowl of ☐

potato chips ☐

a bag of ☐

🇺🇸	potato chips
🇬🇧	crisps

lemonade ☐

soup ☐

B Listen, say, and number the pictures in **A**.

C Play *What's In It?*

a can of

soup

D Now listen to Vania and Precious. Write the country. Who eats fruit for breakfast?

Botswana **Indonesia**

a

Vania

b

Precious

E Listen again. Choose.

1 Vania's favorite fruit is green / brown.

2 It's the king / queen of fruit.

3 You can make cookies / ice cream with durian.

4 The kiwano melon is yellow / green inside.

5 Precious often has melon in a bowl of fruit / soup.

Do you have the same fruit in your country? Why is it important to eat fruit?

Explore Language

A Listen and read. What food does Elena have?

B Look at **A**. Complete.

How Much/Many ..? Some/Any

How	much	food	do we have?	We	have	______	food.
	______	apples		We	don't have	______	lunch.

Remember

any with negative = *no*

C Think and discuss. Then choose.

1 We use *how much* / *how many* to ask about count nouns.
2 We use *how much* / *how many* to ask about noncount nouns.

D Listen and say.

E Look and complete.

~~How much~~ **How many** **some** **any** **How much**

Jack: 1 How much food do we have for the picnic?

Emma: We have 2 ______ potato chips.

Jack: 3 ______ bags do we have?

Emma: Four. And we have a box of cookies.

Jack: And to drink? 4 ______ water do we have?

Emma: Two bottles, and we have some lemonade.

But we don't have 5 ______ orange juice.

F Play *That Makes Ten!* Choose how many.
Then ask and answer.

1 soup (2) 4 cupcakes ( )
2 potato chips ( ) 5 cherries ( )
3 lemonade ( ) 6 corn ( )

How much soup do you have?

I have two cans. How many do you have?

I have eight. That makes ten!

Talk About It

A Watch and listen. What fruit does Rob want?

B Watch again. Check (✔) the phrases you hear.

1 ✔ We need some milk.
2 ◯ How about some lemonade?
3 ◯ How many carrots?
4 ◯ What would you like for dinner?
5 ◯ I'd like a lot of chocolate, please.
6 ◯ What about potato chips?
7 ◯ Let's get three bottles of water.
8 ◯ Anything else?

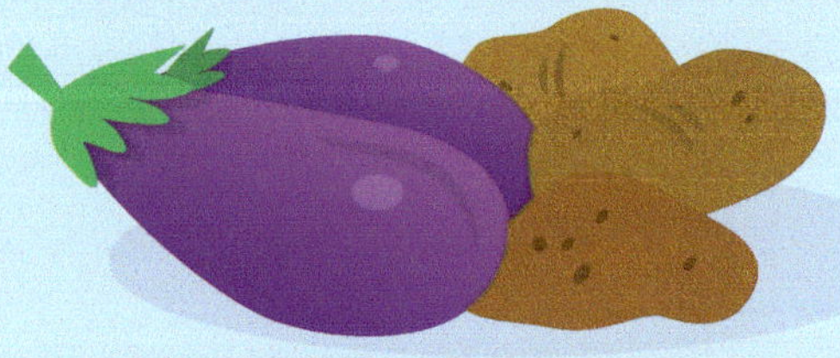

Pronunciation /l/ and /r/

Listen and say.

let's online lemonade Rob carrots rice

What other words do you know with these sounds?

C Plan. You need to go shopping. Write a list.

Shopping List	
lemonade	3 bottles

D Prepare your conversation. Use your ideas from **C** and phrases from **B**.

A

OK, we need ...

B

Ask a question

A

Answer

B

Make a suggestion

A

B

Ask a question

A

E Practice with a friend.

OK, we need three bottles of lemonade.

Reflect
Did we use different ways to make suggestions?
Yes / No

Write About It

A Read the description. Underline the capital letters and circle the commas (,).

Our Kitchen

In the cabinet we have some rice, pasta, and cans of peas. Dad loves peas. We don't have many cupcakes, cookies, and bags of potato chips. On the table there's a bowl of fruit. There are some cherries, apples, and mangos. Mom eats a mango every day. We eat a lot of fruit and vegetables in my family.

B Write the sentences with capital letters and commas.

When do we use capital letters?

1 we eat fruit rice and pasta. We eat fruit, rice, and pasta.

2 carlos likes mangos pasta and cherries.

3 i eat dinner with mom dad and grandpa.

4 she has a lot of soup rice and water.

C Plan. Think about your kitchen and your family. Complete.

We have / don't have ...	Who likes it?

D Draw your kitchen and describe it.

Reflect
Did I use capital letters and commas?

Read the questions and draw or write your answers.

What did I do?

What did I learn?

What was my favorite part?

How well did I do?

What can I do next?

- Watch
- Practice
- Share
- Find out more

Hello! I'm Elena. Where do I go with my class? Find out in Unit 3.

UNIT 1
UNIT 2

Lemonade for Everyone

TELL A STORY

1 Work in pairs.
2 Speaker 1 looks at picture 1 and makes a sentence.
3 Speaker 2 looks at picture 2.
4 Speaker 2 repeats the sentence about picture 1 and makes a sentence about picture 2.
5 Continue and finish the story.

Henry and Leo are using computers in the language lab.

Henry and Leo are using computers in the language lab. Henry says, I always ...

How many sentences can you remember?

Use these words to help you.

computer language lab playground use drink have
play lemonade water bottles of a lot of many much

UNIT 3

It Keeps Changing

A Listen and find. Where's Ivan going?

B Listen, say, and number the pictures in A.

C Listen. Close your eyes and visualize.

D Look and write.

Land	Water
mountain	river

E Listen and sing. Then watch and sing.

It's a Wonderful World

Nature is a wonderful thing.
It's a wonderful world we're living in.
With changing nature everywhere,
It's a wonderful, wonderful world!

Up in the mountains it's very cold.
There are a lot of valleys and waterfalls.
Glaciers can change to beautiful lakes.
It's a wonderful, wonderful world!

Out in the desert it's very hot.
And you need to drink a lot.
Forests can change from green to red.
It's a wonderful, wonderful world!

Explore Language

A Listen and read. Where's Ivan?

B Look at **A**. Complete.

Simple Past: *Be* 1

I	was	behind the tree.	It	______	a lake millions of years ago.
We	______	in the forest.	They	**weren't**	scared.

Look

We can use *ago* with the simple past: *millions of years ago.*

C Think and discuss. Then choose.

1 We use *was* or *were* to talk about the present / past.

D Listen and say.

E Read and complete.

~~was~~ **were** **wasn't** **weren't** **was**

Dear Mom and Dad,

I'm having a great time! Yesterday I **1** ☺ was at the lake. It **2** ☺ ______ very hot, but the water **3** ☹ ______ hot! Jack and Lucy **4** ☹ ______ there because they **5** ☺ ______ on the mountain.

See you soon,
Sam

F Play *Pass the Whisper!*

How do animals change?

A Listen to Sebastian learn about animals. Who's losing hair and skin right now?

B Listen, say, and number the pictures in **A**.

C Play a game. Choose three animals. Describe and guess.

D Now listen to Ingi and Kulap. Write the country. Which animal is now red and blue?

Thailand **Iceland**

a

Ingi ______________

b

Kulap ______________

E Listen again. Check (✔).

1	What does Ingi live near?	a glacier ✔		a desert	
2	What color are arctic foxes in summer?	white		brown	
3	How does their winter fur help them?	to hide		to climb	
4	What animal does Kulap like?	fish		cats	
5	What part of a betta fish changes color?	eyes		scales	

Do animals in your country change their skin? Why do animals change?

Explore Language

A Listen and read. Why are the leaves brown now?

Nita: Hi Ravi. How's Charlie?
Ravi: Umm … I don't know. I can't see him!
Nita: Oh, no!
Ravi: He was here yesterday.
Nita: OK. Where was he yesterday? Was he on those brown leaves?
Ravi: No, he wasn't. Hmm … those leaves weren't brown before.
Nita: Were they green?
Ravi: Yes, they were.
Nita: You see, they were new yesterday. Now they're old.
Ravi: Oh! Look, there he is!
Nita: Where? Oh! Silly Charlie!

B Look at **A**. Complete.

Simple Past: *Be* 2

Where	was	he	yesterday?
	were	the leaves	

______	he	on those brown leaves?	No,	he	______ .
______	they	green?	Yes,	they	______ .

yesterday = the day before today

Look

C Think and discuss. Then choose.

1 We use *was* or *were* to make questions about now / the past.

D Listen and say.

Yesterday, at the animal park:

E Look and complete.

1 What color was the penguin?
It was black and white.

2 ______ the swan white?

No, it ______ . It was green.

3 What color ______ the ducks? They were purple.

4 ______ the snakes green? No, they ______ .

5 ______ the keeper angry? Yes, he ______ .

F Play a memory game. Close your book. Ask and answer with your friend.

What color were the snakes?

Were they purple?

No!

Talk About It

A Watch and listen. What animals do Gus and Lara love?

B Watch again. Match.

1 I was here last summer.
2 They were gray and small before.
3 I love penguins!
4 They were babies, too.
5 I don't like caterpillars.
6 Now they're butterflies!

a. Cool!
b. Me, too.
c. Me, neither.
d. Wow!
e. Amazing!
f. Really?

Pronunciation /ɑr/ and /ʌ/

Listen and say.

park Lara are summer Gus love

What other words do you know with these sounds?

C Plan. What animals do you see at the Safari Park? Complete.

Animal	Before	Now
penguin	small, gray baby	black and white

D Prepare your conversation. Use your ideas from **C** and phrases from **B**.

A

Talk about an animal

Look! There's a ...

Respond and talk about an animal

B

Respond and talk about an animal

E Practice with a friend.

Reflect
Did we sound enthusiastic?
Yes / No

Write About It

A Read the postcard. Underline *but* and circle *and.*

Thursday, June 3

Hi Sofia,
I'm having a great time here. Yesterday, we were at a river near the mountains and it was really hot. This postcard shows you the river millions of years ago. The mountains were the same, but the river was different. It wasn't a river then. It was a glacier and it was clean!
See you soon,
Ana

When do we use *but*?

B Join the sentences with *and* or *but*.

1 I was at a lake. It was very beautiful.

I was at a lake and it was very beautiful.

2 I was hot. The water was cold.

____

3 A baby duck is small. An adult duck is big.

____

4 A polar bear lives in the Arctic. It eats fish.

____

C Plan. Think about a place. Choose and complete.

glacier lake ocean beach desert

hot cold dirty clean big small

Place	Before		Now
		→	
		→	

D Write your postcard. Draw a picture.

Reflect
Did I use *and* or *but*?

Read the questions and draw or write your answers.

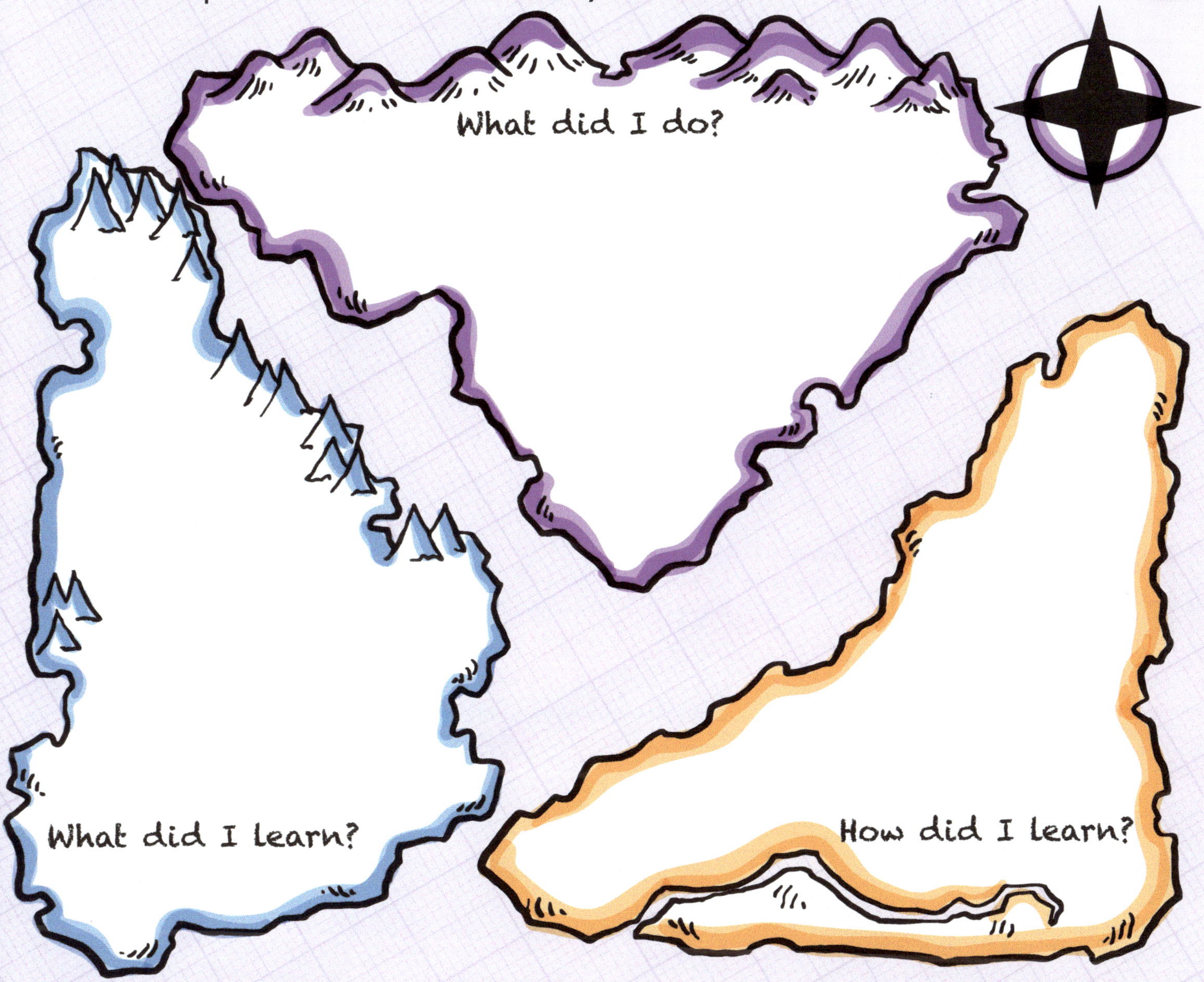

How well did I do?

What can I do next?

- ◯ Read
- ◯ Watch
- ◯ Sing
- ◯ Practice

Hello! I'm Ravi. Who am I with at the school fair? Find out in Unit 4.

UNIT 4

What Happened?

A Listen and find. Who wins the Spelling Bee?

B Listen, say, and number the pictures in A.

C Listen. Close your eyes and visualize.

D Look and write.

1. trip
2.
3.
4.
5.
6.
7.
8.
9.

E Listen and sing. Then watch and sing.

It's OK

It's time for the Spelling Bee.
But I still need to study!
Oh no, I don't think I can win.
Oh no, it's time to begin!

It's OK.
It's fine.
You can do it, friend of mine!

It's time for the cake sale, hurry!
But that's a lot to carry.
Oh no, you can't carry those plates.
Oh no, don't trip and drop the cakes!

It's OK.
It's fine.
You can bake them again in time!

A Listen and read. Who was lucky?

1

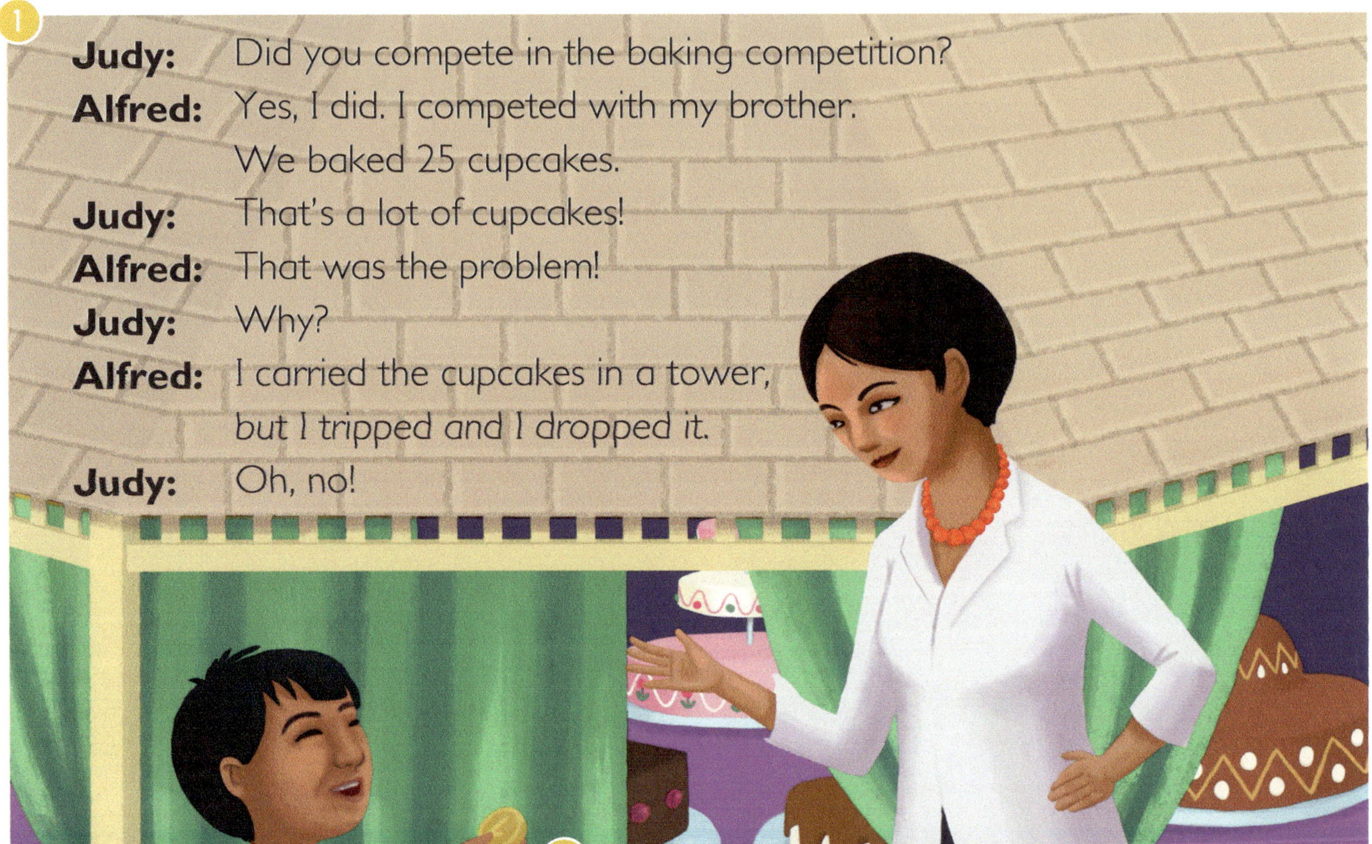

2

Alfred: But … I didn't drop *all* of the cupcakes.
Judy: You were lucky!
Alfred: Yes, but I did drop some!

B Look at A. Complete.

Simple Past: Regular Verbs 1

We	baked	25 cupcakes.	I	**didn't bake**	bread.
I	______	the cupcakes.	She	**didn't carry**	any cakes.
I	______	it.	I	______	all of the cupcakes.

carry → carried,
but play → played

Remember

C Think and discuss. Then choose.

1 We add –es / –ed to regular verbs in sentences about the past.

D Listen and say.

E Read and complete in simple past.

The children 1 competed (compete) in a baking competition. They 2 ______ (not bake) cookies. They 3 ______ (bake) cupcakes. Alfred 4 ______ (carry) the cupcakes to the table. But he 5 ______ (not carry) them well. He tripped and 6 ______ (drop) them! It was very funny!

F Play a chain game. Then write.

I studied English.

He studied English. I baked cupcakes.

I studied English.
Asim baked cupcakes.

What is special about a first day at school?

A Listen to Kadir talk to his brother about his first day at school. When does Kadir start school?

play ☐

travel 1

bounce ☐

practice (US) / practise (UK)

practice ☐

learn ☐

move ☐

smile ☐

pack ☐

finish ☐

wait ☐

B Listen, say, and number the pictures in **A**.

C Play a game. Choose five actions. Mime and guess.

D Now listen to Hiroko and Wati. Write the country.
Who starts school in July?

Indonesia	Japan

a

b

E Listen again. Choose the correct name.

1	There are 35 students in the class.	(Hiroko)	Wati
2	It is her sister's first day.	Hiroko	Wati
3	School starts in April.	Hiroko	Wati
4	There was a big ceremony on the first day.	Hiroko	Wati
5	School starts in July.	Hiroko	Wati

**Was your first day at school the same or different?
Did it feel special? Why?**

A Listen and read. Where do Anna's friends live?

B Look at **A**. Complete.

Simple Past: Regular Verbs 2

______	Anna	pack her backpack?	Yes,	she	______
	we	______ our bikes?	No,	we	didn't.
	you	study in your bedroom?	No,	I	

Did you play football?
not ~~Did you played football?~~
Watch Out

C Think and discuss. Then choose.

1 We use did / do + infinitive verb to make questions in the past.

D Listen and say.

E Put the words in order. Then answer for you.

1 you / yesterday? / Did / ride / your / bike
Did you ride your bike yesterday? ______ Yes, I did.

2 bedroom? / in / you / Did / study / your
______ ______

3 your mom / week? / Did / last / bake / a cake
______ ______

4 Did / friends / your / practice / basketball / yesterday?
______ ______

F Guess about your friends. Then ask and answer.

1 Maria carried a ball yesterday.
2 Ali didn't watch television.

Did you carry a ball yesterday?

No, I didn't!

Take the Stage

A Watch and listen. Where did Gus go?

B Watch again. Check (✔) the phrases you hear.

1. ✔ I want to tell you about an important event in my life.
2. ◯ This event is my first trip to another country.
3. ◯ It happened last summer.
4. ◯ I was with my family.
5. ◯ It was good because I wanted to learn about a new country.
6. ◯ It was difficult because I don't like competing.
7. ◯ Most of the time I was happy because I studied very hard.

Pronunciation /d/ and /t/ or /ɪd/

Listen and say.

traveled practiced helped started visited wanted

What other words do you know with these sounds?

C Plan. Think about an important event. Choose (✔) and complete.

- ◯ my first day at school
- ◯ a big competition
- ◯ a big birthday party
- ◯ passing a big test
- ◯ a family day out
- ◯ a big performance
- ◯ moving to a new house
- ◯ my first visit to another country

When? ______________ Who with? ______________

Actions: ______________ ______________ ______________

Why was it good? ______________

Why was it difficult? ______________

How did you feel? ______________

D Prepare your presentation. Use your ideas from **C** and phrases from **B**.

Introduce your presentation *Hello, I want to tell you about ...*

____

Talk about your important event ______________

____

____

____

____

Finish ______________

E Practice with a friend. Then share with your class.

Reflect
Did I look at the audience?
Yes / No

Write About It

A Read the event description. Circle the regular verb endings.

Last week something awesome happened! I was in a race at school. I started at the front of the race, but I tripped. My friend was next to me. She stopped and helped me. She was really kind. We didn't finish first, but we finished the race together. I learned that she's a really good friend!

B Look at **A** and the regular verbs in the box. Complete.

~~happen~~ ~~trip~~ bounce stop learn study ~~carry~~ ~~compete~~

+ –d	+ –ed	+ consonant + –ed	~~y~~ + –ied
competed	happened	tripped	carried

C Plan. Think about something you learned from an event. Choose and complete.

What happened? Something funny / amazing / good / sad / happy

Where? ____________________

When? ____________________

Who were you with? ____________________

Actions: __________ __________ __________

I learned that: ____________________

Reflect
Did I check my spelling for regular verbs in the simple past?

D Write your event description.

Read the questions and draw or write your answers.

What did I do?

What did I learn?

What was my favorite part?

How well did I do?

What can I do next?

- Share
- Play
- Talk
- Find out more

Hello! I'm Anna. What do I see at the museum? Find out in Unit 5.

UNIT 3

UNIT 4

Explore The Island

HOW TO PLAY

1 Prepare the cards, the counters and the spinner. Then choose your home.
2 Use your spinner to move around the board.
3 Stop on the same square as your friend. Your friend goes home.
4 The winner is the first person to get to the island.

UNIT 5

Let's Go Back

A Listen and find. What's David's favorite dinosaur?

B Listen, say, and number the pictures in **A**.

C Listen. Close your eyes and visualize.

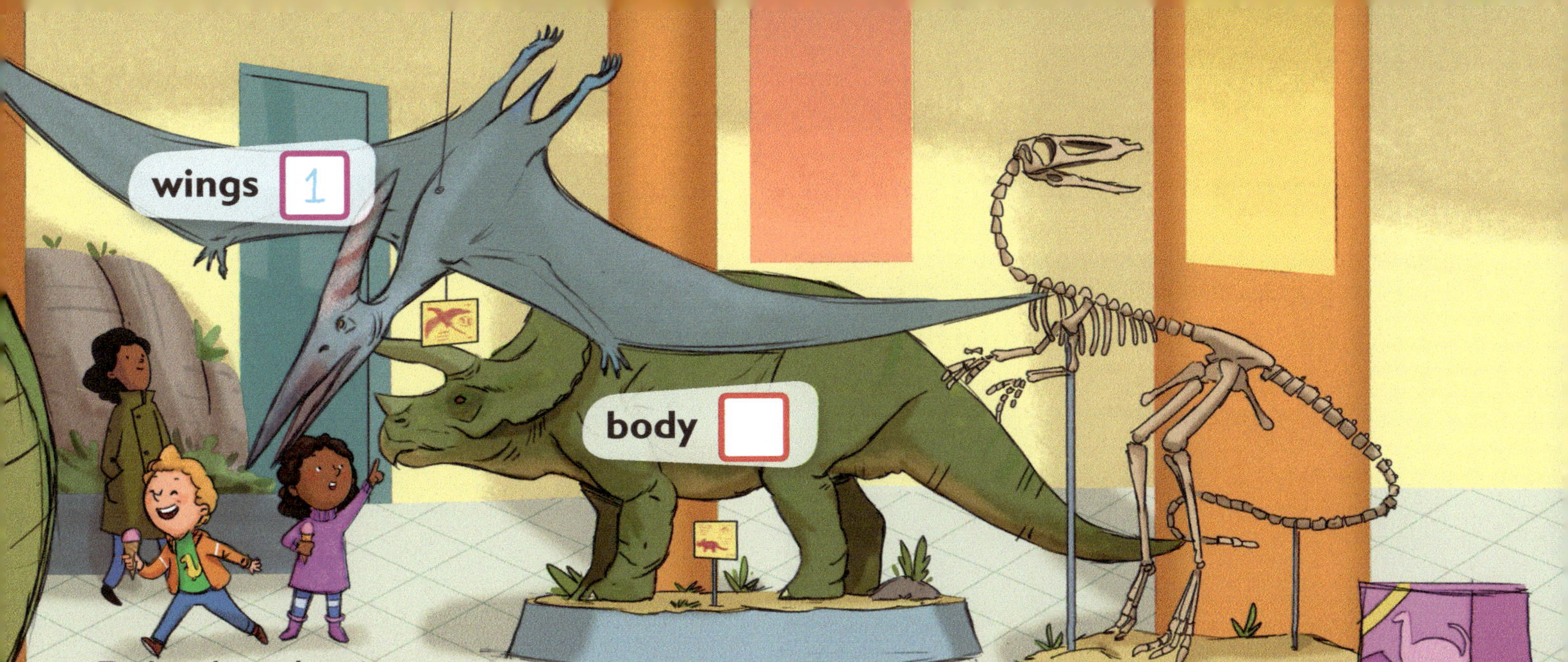

D Look and write.

Animal Words	Descriptions
wings	dangerous

E Listen and sing. Then watch and sing.

King of the Dinosaurs

T-Rex, T-Rex,
King of the dinosaurs,
T-Rex, T-Rex,
Roar! Roar! Roar!

It had a huge body and a great big head,
Its mouth was full of scary teeth.
It had a long tail, two short arms,
And claws on its fingers and feet.

It wasn't fast, but it wasn't slow,
It walked on its two back legs.
It didn't have wings – it wasn't a bird.
But it started life as an egg.

A Listen and read. Did the dinosaur eat meat?

B Look at A. Complete.

Simple Past: Irregular Verbs 1

I	saw	it there.	You	**didn't see**	the dinosaur.
We	______	to the dinosaur exhibition.	They	**didn't go**	to the shop.
It	______	meat.	It	______	plants.

Remember

He saw it. not ~~He saws it.~~

C Think and discuss. Then choose.

1 We use the simple past to talk about events before / after now.

2 Regular / Irregular verbs have different forms.

D Listen and say.

E Read and complete in simple past.

We 1 went (go) to the Science Museum yesterday. I 2 ______ (see) a dinosaur. It 3 ______ (have) huge claws! It 4 ______ (not have) a big tail. These dinosaurs 5 ______ (run) very quickly and they 6 ______ (not eat) meat.

F Play *Tic Tac Toe*.

Two years ago, I went to a museum.

Yesterday / have	Last year / go	This morning / see
Last weekend / eat	On Saturday / drink	Last month / run
Three months ago / have	Yesterday / see	Two years ago / go

Where can we learn about the past in different countries?

A Listen to Paz talk about a museum near her town. What was very dirty there?

B Listen, say, and number the pictures in **A**.

C Play *Back Spelling*. Guess the words your friend is spelling.

D Now listen to Karol and Rashid. Number the pictures.
Who lives in an old city?

a

Rashid, Pakistan ☐

b

Karol, Poland ☐

E Listen again. Write *True* or *False*.

1 Karol visited a museum. True

2 He saw a dinosaur skeleton. ______

3 He didn't like the museum. ______

4 Rashid's city isn't very old. ______

5 His dad works at a museum. ______

Which place do you want to visit? Why?
Where can you learn about the past in your country?

Explore Language

A Listen and read. What were the interesting shapes?

1

Harold: Look, Jannah! Yesterday, we used this digital scanner.

Jannah: Really? What did you see?

Harold: We saw these interesting shapes.

Jannah: Wow! Did you dig there?

Harold: Yes, we did. We dug for hours.

Jannah: What did you find?

Harold: We found three cans and an old plate.

Jannah: Oh! What did you learn from that?

Harold: We learned that dinosaurs liked to have parties!

Jannah: Oh, Dad!

2

B Look at **A**. Complete.

Simple Past: Irregular Verbs 2

What	did	you	see?

______	you	dig?	______	we	did.
			No,	I	______

What ...? asks for specific information.

Remember

C Think and discuss. Then choose.

1 Questions with *What did ... ?* and *Did ... ?* ask about the past / present.

D Listen and say.

E Put the words in order.

Dee: This is Chloe. She found something in her garden last week.
1 What did you find, Chloe? (What / you / did / find)

Chloe: I found a dinosaur fossil!

Dee: 2 ______ it? (did / Where / you / find)

Chloe: It was under a tree in my garden.

Dee: 3 ______? (you / find it / Did)

Chloe: No, I didn't, it was my dog.

Dee: 4 ______ it was a fossil? (you / Did / know)

Chloe: No, I didn't. I thought it was my dog's bone!

F Play *Back to the Board*. Say answers for your friend to guess the question.

I found an old jug.

I found a skeleton!

I found a dinosaur bone.

Take the Stage

A Watch and listen. What did Flo's dinosaur eat?

B Watch again. Check (✔) the phrases you hear.

1 (✔) I'm going to talk about the Floraptor.

2 ( ) It was like a swan, my favorite animal.

3 ( ) It wasn't like a lizard.

4 ( ) It had scales like a lizard.

5 ( ) It didn't have wings.

6 ( ) It was very scary.

7 ( ) It had a tiny mouth.

8 ( ) It was a cool dinosaur!

Pronunciation /oʊ/ and /ɔr/

Listen and say.

nose slow Ecuador dinos**aur**

What other words do you know with these sounds?

C **Plan. Invent your dinosaur. Write and choose (✓).**

What was its name? ____________

Where did it live? ____________

When did it live? ____________

What other animal was it like? ____________

◯ huge ◯ small
◯ quick ◯ slow ◯ dangerous
◯ scary ◯ cool ◯ body ◯ tail
◯ teeth ◯ wings ◯ claws

D **Prepare your presentation. Use your ideas from C and phrases from B.**

Introduce your presentation *Hi, I'm going to talk about ...*

____

Talk about your dinosaur ____________

____

____

____

____

Finish ____________

E **Practice with a friend. Then share with your class.**

Reflect
Did I clearly show my picture?
Yes / No

Write About It

A Read the diary. Underline *because* and the phrase after it.

Monday, September 10

Last Saturday I went to the Kids' Dig Camp. In the morning, we saw a video. I liked it because it was about Mexico. In the afternoon, we walked to a beach for our dig. We dug slowly because the pottery was very old. I found some beautiful bowls, but I didn't find any jugs. Some bowls were broken because they were 200 years old.

When do we use *because*?

B Match.

1 I studied English
2 We didn't climb the mountain
3 The monkey ate five bananas
4 I went to the park
5 She danced to the song

a. because she liked the music.
b. because I wanted to ride my scooter.
c. because the weather was bad.
d. because I had an exam.
e. because it was hungry.

C Plan. Think about last Saturday. Complete.

What did you do?	Why?

D Write about last Saturday. Draw a picture.

Reflect
Did I use *because* to give information and a reason?

Read the questions and draw or write your answers.

What did I do?

What did I learn?

How did I learn?

How well did I do?

What can I do next?

- Read
- Practice
- Play
- Find out more

Hello! I'm Harold. What do I see in Art Class? Find out in Unit 6.

UNIT 6

Look What I Made

A Listen and find. What color are Mr. Pocassi's eyes?

B Listen, say, and number the pictures in A.

C Listen. Close your eyes and visualize.

Recycle

D Look and write.

1 curly

2

3

4

5

6

7

8

9

10

E Listen and sing. Then watch and sing.

Get Creative

Get creative! Have some fun!
Get creative, everyone!

Don't sit there and watch TV.
Make a painting, play with me.
Do a drawing, bake a cake.
There are a lot of things to make.

Don't sit there and wait all day.
Make some jewelry, that's the way!
Make a sculpture with a box.
Make a toy with old socks.

🇺🇸 jewelry
mustache

🇬🇧 jewellery
moustache

A Listen and read. Who did Lizzy paint?

B Look at **A**. Complete.

Comparatives 1

The hands	are	bigger		Dad's.
The hair	is	______	______	Dad's.
My painting	______	______		yours.

Some adjectives are irregular:
bad = *worse than*, not ~~*badder than*~~

Watch Out

C Think and discuss. Then choose.

1 We use comparative adjectives to describe the differences between two / more than two things or people.

D Listen and say.

E Look and complete.

happy **curly** **young** **sad** ~~**old**~~ **straight**

1 Helen is older than Paul.
2 Carla is ______ Stefan.
3 Ingrid's hair is ______ Igor's hair.
4 Helen's hair is ______ Stefan's.
5 Carla is ______ Paul.
6 Harry is ______ Carla.

F Play *Guess Who!* Look, say, and guess.

His hair is shorter than Ingrid's.

Is it Paul?

Yes!

Which famous places in the world are amazing?

A Listen to Sara talk about how she likes making things. Where's Sara's favorite place?

quiet 1

noisy

new

thick

hard

wall

messy

building

soft

clean

clean (US) / tidy (UK)

B Listen, say, and number the pictures in **A**.

C Play *The Adjectives Game*.

D Now listen to Thomas and Natasha. Number the pictures. Who visited a museum?

a

Thomas, Belgium ☐

b

Natasha, Russia ☐

E Listen again. Choose.

1 Kizhi Island is on a big lake / the sea.

2 It has a lot of different animals / buildings.

3 Natasha made a model / drawing for her history project.

4 Thomas loves art / science.

5 Thomas made a model / drawing of it.

What are some famous places in your country? How do people feel about them? Why?

A Listen and read. Why is Lizzy happy?

B Look at **A**. Complete.

Superlatives 1

They	're		smallest	buildings.
This fair	is	______	______	place.
That	's		______	model.

Remember

Some adjectives are irregular:
bad → *the worst*, not ~~*the baddest*~~

C Think and discuss. Then choose.

1 We use superlative adjectives to compare two / more than two things or people.

D Listen and say.

E Look at **A**. Complete with superlative adjectives.

tall good cool noisy ~~small~~

1 The shops are the smallest buildings.

2 Nathan says the fair is ______ place.

3 Joe says the fair is ______ place.

4 Nathan says Lizzy's mountain is ______ model.

5 Joe says the mountain is ______ model.

6 I think ______.

F Look in your book. Find and write.

1 cool / page

2 tall / person

3 good / activity

4 cute / person

5 small / picture

The coolest page is page 36!

Take the Stage

A Watch and listen. Who does Greta make a picture of?

B Watch again. Check (✔) the phrases you hear.

1 ☑ I'm going to show you how to make a collage.
2 ◯ Choose your materials.
3 ◯ You need scissors and glue.
4 ◯ Use a pencil (or crayon) and draw your face.
5 ◯ Cut out your face shape.
6 ◯ You can decorate it with colors.
7 ◯ My collage has different colored paper.
8 ◯ Finally, it's finished.
9 ◯ Here's my portrait.

Pronunciation /g/ and /k/

Listen and say.

Greta going glue collage color cut

What other words do you know with these sounds?

C Plan. Think of a collage you can make. Choose (✓) or write.

What is it?	◯ a portrait ◯ a monster ◯ a toy ◯ a place in your home town ◯ ________
Materials	◯ paints ◯ colored paper ◯ stickers ◯ glue ◯ shells ◯ scissors ◯ ________
Actions	◯ draw ◯ cut out ◯ paint ◯ color ◯ use ◯ decorate with ◯ ________

D Prepare your presentation. Use your ideas from **C** and phrases from **B**.

Introduce your presentation Hi, I'm going to show you how to ...

____

Talk about your collage ____

____

____

____

____

Finish ____

E Practice with a friend. Then share with your class.

Hi, I'm going to show you how to make a monster.

Reflect
Did I organize my ideas clearly?
Yes / No

Write About It

A Read the personal profile. Circle the comparative adjectives. Underline the superlative adjectives.

All About Me

Name: Modelia Age: 7

Description: I have brown curly hair. My hair is curlier than my brother's. His name is Modifi. He's older than me, but my bedroom is bigger than his. My favorite activity is dancing. I'm the shortest in my family, but I'm the best dancer.

B Look at **A**. Write the adjectives in the table.

noisy short big bad good old curly hot

	Comparatives	Superlatives
+ –*er*/+ –*est*	shorter,	
+ consonant + –*er*/+ –*est*		biggest,
–y + –*ier*/+ –*iest*		curliest,
irregular	better,	

C Plan. Think about yourself. Complete.

Name: ________ Hair: ________ Adjective: ________

Age: ________ Activity: ________

Reflect
Did I check my spelling for comparative and superlative adjectives?

D Write your personal profile.

Read the questions and draw or write your answers.

What did I do?

What did I learn?

What was my favorite part?

How well did I do?

What can I do next?

- Watch
- Practice
- Share
- Find out more

Hello! I'm Joe.
What activity is my team doing?
Find out in Unit 7.

UNIT 5
UNIT 6

Race to the Museum!

HOW TO PLAY

1 Make counters. Use your spinner to move around the board.
2 Look at the picture where you land.
3 Make sentences.
4 The winner is the first person to get to the museum.

What did you see?
Say three things.
scary
elephant
dinosaur
tiger
What did they drink?
Say three things.
What did they eat?
Say three things.
hat did you
nd? Say three
things.
You tripped on
a bone.
GO BACK 4
SPACES.
dirty
Jug 1
Jug 2
Jug 3
Describe
the picture.
Pippa
noisy
chameleon
snake
lion
Oh no, it's a
T-Rex!
MISS A TURN.
Where did
she go on
vacation?
Describe the
picture.
FINISH
MUSEUM
You dropped a fossil.
GO BACK 4
SPACES.

UNIT 7

We're a Team

A Listen and find. Who loves singing?

B Listen, say, and number the pictures in **A**.

C Listen. Close your eyes and visualize.

yoga 1

skating

singing

D Look and write.

1 kayaking

2

3

4

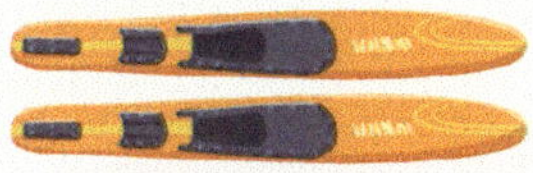
5

6

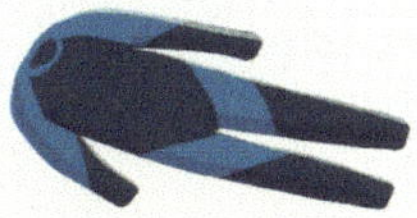
7

8

9

10

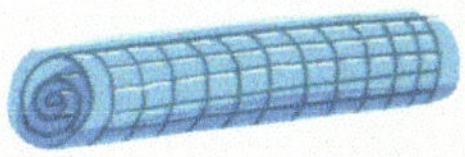
11

E Listen and sing. Then watch and sing.

Teamwork is Number One

What do you do as a team, team, team?
What do you do for fun?
We're all good at different things,
But teamwork is number one!

I'm good at acting.
I'm good at singing.
Together we can do a show!
I like windsurfing.
Can you teach me?
Yes! Together we can go, go, go.

I'm good at biking.
And horseback riding.
Together we can ride fast or slow.
I like skating.
Can you teach me?
Yes! Together we can go, go, go.

A Listen and read. Who helps Padma?

B Look at A. Complete.

Telling the Time

What	time		is			it?
	It's	________ .		It's		________ .
	It's	________ .		Dinner is	________	________ .

Look

The "hands" on a clock tell you the time.

C Think and discuss. Then choose.

1 We use the long hand on a clock to tell the hour / minutes.

2 We use the short hand on a clock to tell the hour / minutes.

D Listen and say.

E Look and complete.

Padma: Imran, what 1 time is it?

Imran: It's 10:30. 2 ________ time is kayaking?

Padma: Kayaking is 3 ________ .

Imran: OK. What time is horseback riding?

Padma: It's 4 ________ . What can we do now?

Imran: Skating is 5 ________ .

Padma: Let's go!

F Play a game. Mime and guess.

What time is it?

It's 3 o'clock.

How do people work as a team in different communities?

A Listen to Mr. Muller talk to Zoe and her friends about a garden project. What does Zoe have for the garden?

take turns ☐

share ☐

trade ☐

trade (US) / swap (UK)

borrow ☐

work together ☐

give ☐

help each other ☐

club 1

community ☐

B Listen, say, and number the pictures in **A**.

C Who do you work in a team with and how? Make a list. Tell your friend.

D Now listen to Maia and Bradley. Write the country.
Who played on the playground today?

UK **Myanmar**

a

Maia

b

Bradley

E Listen again. Choose.

1 Bradley did a project at school / a club.

2 Bradley wrote books / letters with another school.

3 He shared ideas by talking on the cell phone / computer.

4 Before, Maia's playground was very dirty / dangerous.

5 The village worked together and built / painted a fence.

Do you have the same team projects in your community? How can you be a good team member?

A Listen and read. Why is Imran in the water?

B Look at **A**. Complete.

Can

Permission			Offers		
Can	we	**borrow** this kayak?	______	I	**help** you?
You	______	**use** it for the next hour.	I	______	**help** you.

Requests		
______	you	**go** quickly?

Remember

I can play not ~~*I can to play.*~~

C Think and discuss. Then choose.

1 We use the verb *can* to say you want / don't like something.

2 We use the verb *can* to say you want to help / say the time.

D Listen and say.

E Put the words in order.

1 help / me / you / Can Can you help me ?

2 can't / a pen / use / You ______ .

3 we / cards / Can / borrow ______ ?

4 work / we / together / Can ______ ?

5 in the classroom / We / run / can't ______ .

6 to write / You / can / take turns / on the whiteboard

______ ______ .

F Play *You're the Teacher!*

Can I go to the bathroom?

Yes, you can.

Talk About It

A Watch and listen. Why do Jason and Grace choose sailing?

Watch
Who do they look at when they're speaking?

B Watch again. Check (✔) the phrases you hear.

1 (✔) I know, let's do an outdoor activity.
2 ( ) How about mountain climbing?
3 ( ) I'm not sure about climbing.
4 ( ) Do you like watersports?
5 ( ) OK. What do you want to do?
6 ( ) Which do you prefer?
7 ( ) I prefer sailing because it's really fun.

Pronunciation /n/ and /ŋ/

Listen and say.

Jason mountain open climbing morning sailing

What other words do you know with these sounds?

C Plan. Think about activities you want to do. Choose and write.

Activity	Do you want to do it?	Why?
sailing	yes / no	It's a team activity.
	yes / no	
	yes / no	
	yes / no	

D Prepare your conversation. Use your ideas from **C** and phrases from **B**.

A

What can we do on Saturday?

Give your opinion and make a suggestion

Give your opinion

Great!

B

Make a suggestion

Give your opinion and make a suggestion

OK. Let's

Reflect
Did I look at my friend?
Yes / No

E Practice with a friend.

Write About It

A Read the team game instructions. Circle the imperative verbs.

My Favorite Team Game
My favorite team game is called "Team Catch."
This is how you play it:

- Run quickly!
- Catch a player.
- Hold hands and make a team.
- Don't stop!
- Catch more players.
- Do you have the biggest team? You win!

I like this game because I can run quickly and I like to work together with my team.

Is there a subject in the imperative sentences?

B Write the imperative sentences.

1 ☺ sing / a song Sing a song.

2 ☹ watch / TV Don't ____________

3 ☺ help / your friend ____________

4 ☹ drop / the ball ____________

5 ☺ bounce / the ball ____________

6 ☹ move ____________

C Plan. Think about a team game. Choose or write.

Game:
- treasure hunt
- soccer
- ____________

Why I like it:
____

Actions:
- run
- find
- kick
- ____________

D Write your team game instructions.

Reflect
Did I use imperative verbs?

Read the questions and draw or write your answers.

How well did I do?

What can I do next?

- Read
- Talk
- Watch
- Find out more

Hello! I'm Susan. What sport do I play? Find out in Unit 8.

UNIT 8

You're My Hero

A Listen and find. Does Mom win?

B Listen, say, and number the pictures in A.

C Listen. Close your eyes and visualize.

🇺🇸	🇬🇧
track and field	athletics

D Look and write.

Sports	Adjectives
tennis	popular

E Listen and sing. Then watch and sing.

Who's Your Hero?

Who's your hero?
Is it a sports hero?
Who's your hero?
Shout out the name.

Do they play tennis,
Soccer, or volleyball?
Do they do gymnastics,
Or play basketball?

Who's my sports hero?
It's difficult to say.
Sports are so exciting,
In many different ways.

Explore Language

A Listen and read. Who's the hero?

1

Dad:	That looks exciting. Is it your homework?
Bob:	No, it's more exciting than homework. I'm making a poster about my hero.
Dad:	Oh, so who's your hero?
Bob:	It's a secret.
Dad:	Hmmm. Is he popular?
Bob:	He's more popular than my favorite actor.
Dad:	Is he strong?
Bob:	He's *stronger than … an elephant.*
Dad:	Oh, this is difficult.
Bob:	Yes, it's more difficult than my math homework!
Dad:	Is it me?

math
maths

2

Bob:	Noooo! Look! It's The Human Elephant!
Dad:	Oh!

B Look at **A**. Complete.

Comparatives 2

It	's		exciting		homework.
He	's	______	______	______	my favorite actor.
It	's		______		my math homework.

more exciting than
not ~~*excitinger than*~~
Look

C **Think and discuss. Then choose.**

1 We use comparatives to describe the differences between two / more than two things.

2 We add *more* when the adjective has one syllable / two or more syllables.

D **Listen and say.**

E **Put the words in order. Do you agree (✔) or disagree (✗)?**

1 Gymnastics / difficult / volleyball. / is / than / more
Gymnastics is more difficult than volleyball. ◯

2 Track and field / is / exciting / more / basketball. / than
______ ◯

3 is / Tennis / than / more / popular / table tennis.
______ ◯

4 Karate / than / dangerous / is / more / swimming.
______ ◯

F Choose and say.

gymnastics, table tennis, yoga, acting, waterskiing, hockey, karate, kayaking, surfing

Waterskiing is more dangerous than kayaking!

No, it isn't. Kayaking is more dangerous than waterskiing!

Who are heroes around the world?

A Listen to Felipe talk about his hero. Who's his hero?

helpful ☐

friendly ☐

interesting ☐

mean ☐

selfish ☐

brave ☐

intelligent ☐

beautiful ☐

thoughtful 1

B Listen, say, and number the pictures in **A**.

C Play *Back Spelling*. Guess the words your friend is spelling.

D Now listen to Mónica and Shayma. Number the pictures. Whose hero is strong?

a

Shayma, Tunisia ☐

b

Mónica, Cuba ☐

E Listen again. Choose the correct name.

1 She loves reading. — (Mónica) — Shayma

2 Her hero writes books. — Mónica — Shayma

3 Her favorite sport is track and field. — Mónica — Shayma

4 Her hero is a very quick runner. — Mónica — Shayma

5 She likes stories about her country. — Mónica — Shayma

Who are your heroes from your country? Why are they heroes?

A Listen and read. Why is the teacher intelligent?

B Look at A. Complete.

Superlatives 2

He	is	______	______	______	student.
She	's	______	______	intelligent	teacher.
English	is			______	class.

Look

the most helpful
not ~~the helpfulest~~

C Think and discuss. Then choose.

1 We use superlative adjectives to describe the differences between two / more than two things.

2 We add *the most* when the adjective has one syllable / two or more syllables.

D Listen and say.

E Choose and write.

helpful thoughtful interesting intelligent ~~patient~~

1 John is the most patient person in the class.

2 ______ person in my family.

3 ______ person in my town.

4 ______ person in my country.

5 ______ person in the world!

F Choose and say.

difficult sport dangerous animals important person exciting activity popular book

I think gymnastics is the most difficult sport.

Me too!

Talk About It

A Watch and listen. What is Lara's superhero's name?

B Watch again. Check (✓) the phrases you hear.

1 ✓ Don't let me see yours!
2 ◯ Ready?
3 ◯ You go first.
4 ◯ You play Fun Fifi.
5 ◯ What score does Top Tim have for 'kind'?
6 ◯ I win.
7 ◯ Is it your turn?
8 ◯ It's my turn.

Pronunciation /oʊ/ and /aʊ/

Listen and say.

OK go so how now wow

What other words do you know with these sounds?

C Plan. You're going to play the Superhero Game. Choose adjectives for the cards.

intelligent   brave   kind   quick   strong

Fun Fifi	
brave	3
______	4
______	6
______	8
______	9

Super Sam	
______	3
______	4
______	6
______	8
______	9

Top Tanya	
______	3
______	4
______	6
______	8
______	9

Awesome Ali	
______	3
______	4
______	6
______	8
______	9

Neat Nina	
______	3
______	4
______	6
______	8
______	9

Big Bob	
______	3
______	4
______	6
______	8
______	9

D Now, play the game. Use your cards from **C** and phrases from **B**.

You go first. Choose an adjective.

Hmm ... 'brave'. And you play *Fun Fifi*.

OK. You play *Super Sam*. What score does he have for 'brave'?

He has 9. What score does *Fun Fifi* have?

She has 6 ... You win this round!

Reflect

Did I use a new word or phrase?

Yes / No

Write About It

A Read the hero profile. Underline *I think* and the word after it. Circle *because*.

My Grandpa

This is my grandpa. I think he's the most awesome person because he can do a lot of things. He plays volleyball with his friends. It's a difficult sport. I think he plays better than my dad. He plays games with me and he reads me stories. I love his stories because they're funny. I think he's the kindest person because he takes care of me. He's the best grandpa!

How can we give our opinion?

B Match.

1 I play basketball because

2 My younger brother

3 I think my mom does yoga

4 We think tigers

a. thinks painting is difficult.

b. are the most dangerous animals.

c. because she likes it.

d. it's the most exciting sport.

C Plan. Think about your hero. Choose and complete.

My Hero

Who

____

Personality

kind / brave / intelligent / helpful / thoughtful / friendly / interesting / fantastic

Why? ______________________

____

Activities

____

____

D Write a hero profile.

Reflect
Did I give my opinion?

Read the questions and draw or write your answers.

What did I do?

What did I learn?

What was my favorite part?

How well did I do?

What can I do next?

- ◯ Sing
- ◯ Practice
- ◯ Play
- ◯ Share

Hello! I'm Matilde. What place am I visiting? Find out in Unit 9.

UNIT 7
UNIT 8

Give Me a Clue!

24 I love this game. It's …! **E**

25

26 You need a  to play this sport. **V**

23 You need a  to do this activity. **T**

22

21 This person knows a lot of things and is good at learnin She's … **I**

12 This person always thinks of ways to make people happy. He's ... **T**

13

14 This person doesn't share. He's … **S**

11 I skated first. You skated next. What did we do? **TT**

10 In this sport, you can run, throw, and jump. **TF**

9

START

1 In this activity you can go up mountains, walls, and trees. **C**

2 This person smiles and is kind. He's … **F**

HOW TO PLAY

1 Make counters. Use your spinner to move around the board.
2 Read the clue and say the word starting with the letter.
3 Go up the climbing wall. Go down the river.
4 The winner is the first person to get to the finish.

27 You can use my pencil. I'll let you ____________ it. **B**

28 A lot of things aren't scary for this person. She's … **B**

FINISH

20 You need a to do this activity. **HR**

19

18

15

16 A lot of people like soccer. It's a ____________ game. **P**

17

8 You need to do this activity. **S**

7

6 In this activity you learn songs. **S**

3 ave you a blue ball. You gave me a green ball. What did we do? **T**

4

5 Some people think math is … **D**

UNIT 9

Do You Live Here?

A Listen and find. What does Arni do?

B Listen, say, and number the pictures in A.

C Listen. Close your eyes and visualize.

D Look and write.

Places	Things
stairs	closet

E **Listen and sing. Then watch and sing.**

In the Scary Castle

In the scary castle,
There's a mouse in the fridge,
A spider in the bathtub,
And noises everywhere!

In the scary castle,
There's a bird in the closet,
A mouse in the fridge …

In the scary castle,
There's a bat on the stove,
A bird in the closet …

In the scary castle,
There's a skeleton in the attic,
A bat on the stove …

Wooooahhhhhhh!

A Listen and read. What game did Hilda play?

B Look at A. Complete.

Simple Past Review

Regular			Irregular		
We	visited	them.	They	______	me.
I	didn't visit	a museum.	I	______	them.
Did they	visit	a castle?	______ you	find	them?

Did you see it?
not ~~Did you saw it?~~
Remember

C Think and discuss. Then choose.

1 We use the simple past to talk about completed actions in the past / present.

D Listen and say.

E Read and complete.

1 Where did you go (go) on your vacation?
We ______ (visit) a castle.

2 ______ you ______ (climb) the tower?
No, I ______ . It was scary!

3 ______ you ______ (see) your cousin?
Yes, I did. We ______ (play) a game.

4 What game ______ you ______ (play)?
I looked for my cousin, but I ______ (not find) him!

F Play *True or False*. Write sentences. Then ask and answer.

My family and I went to a castle.
I didn't visit a museum last weekend.
______

Did you go to a castle last year?

No, I didn't! It's false!

Why do people visit castles?

A Listen to Shane talk about a castle visit. Did he have fun there?

- frightened ☐
- bored ☐
- annoyed ☐
- sad ☐
- tired ☐
- angry ☐
- proud ☐
- surprised ☐
- happy 1
- excited ☐

B Listen, say, and number the pictures in **A**.

C Play *What Am I Feeling?* Mime and guess.

D Now listen to Min-Seo and Boris. Write the country. Which castle has four towers?

South Korea **Bulgaria**

a

Boris

______

b

Min-Seo

______

E Listen again. Write *True* or *False*.

1 Boris is from Bulgaria. True

2 Baba Vida Castle has five towers. ______

3 There are special events there in the summer. ______

4 Gyeongbok Palace is in South Korea. ______

5 The king didn't live in Gyeongbok Palace. ______

Are there any castles in your country? What can you learn from them?

Explore Language

A Listen and read. Does the castle have a TV?

1

Rolf: Come into this room. It was the great hall.

Carol: Wow! It's huge.

Rolf: There weren't any TVs or computers, but the children weren't bored.

Carol: What did they do?

Rolf: They danced and sang. They watched plays and played music. They were happy.

Carol: Where was the kitchen?

Rolf: Well, there were three kitchens. They were down the stairs, in the basement.

Carol: Was there a bathroom?

Rolf: No, there wasn't.

Carol: Oh, no! I need the bathroom.

Rolf: It's OK, there's a bathroom here now!

B Look at **A**. Complete.

Simple Past: *There Was / There Were*

There	was	a kitchen.	There	were	three kitchens.
There	wasn't	a bathroom.	______	______	any TVs.
______	there	a bathroom?	Yes, ______ was.		
Were	there	any TVs?	No, there weren't.		

Watch Out

There were towers, not ~~*They were towers*~~

C Think and discuss. Then choose.

1 We use *there was* or *there were* to describe things in the present / past.

D Listen and say.

E Look and complete.

1 There were four lamps.

2 ______________ any TVs.

3 ______________ a table.

4 ______________ a computer.

5 ______________ any sofas?

6 Yes, ______________ .

F Play a memory game. Close your book. Ask and answer with a friend.

Were there any lamps?

Yes, there were! There was one next to the sofa.

A Watch and listen. Where's the tennis court?

B Watch again. Match.

1 I'm going to talk about
2 This is
3 There are a lot of toys
4 I have a swimming pool
5 It has a big table
6 There's a tennis court

a. because I want to be a tennis player.
b. my dream house.
c. my tower.
d. so I can share with all my friends.
e. because I love swimming.
f. so I can eat with all my family.

Pronunciation /s/ and /ð/

Listen and say.

Sam · so · swimming · this · the · there

What other words do you know with these sounds?

C Plan. Think about your dream house. Choose (✓) and complete.

What dream rooms do you have?

◯ living room ◯ dining room ◯ kitchen ◯ bathroom

◯ bedroom ◯ basement ◯ ______ ◯ ______

What do you want in your rooms and yard?

◯ toys ◯ TV ◯ tennis court ◯ swimming pool

◯ ______ ◯ ______ ◯ ______ ◯ ______

Why?

____

____

D Prepare your presentation. Use your ideas from **C** and phrases from **B**.

Introduce your presentation _Hi, I'm going to talk about ..._

____

Talk about your dream house ______________________________

____

____

____

____

Finish ______________________________

E Practice with a friend. Then share with your class.

Reflect
Did I look at the audience?
Yes / No

Write About It

A Read the picture story. Underline the beginning phrases for each picture.

One day, I saw an old castle in the forest. I was surprised. My friend Ron wanted to look inside.

First, we ran to the big door and we opened it. There was music inside!

Then, we walked into the huge hallway. We heard laughing.

Finally, we climbed the tall tower and saw ... a party!

What can sequencers tell us?

B Look at **A**. Complete with sequencers. Put the sentences in order.

a Finally, we climbed the tall tower. [4]

b ________, we walked into the huge hallway. [ ]

c ________, we ran to the big door. [ ]

d ________, I saw an old castle. [ ]

C Plan. Think about this story. Make a list of verbs and adjectives.

D Write your picture story.

Reflect
Did I use sequencers?

Read the questions and draw or write your answers.

What did I do?

What did I learn?

How did I learn?

How well did I do?

What can I do next?

- Read
- Share
- Watch
- Play

Hello! I'm Carol. Where am I going with my family? Find out in Unit 10.

UNIT 10

Are We There Yet?

A Listen and find. When is the family's trip?

B Listen, say, and number the pictures in A.

C Listen. Close your eyes and visualize.

D Look and write.

Getting ready	Getting there	Places
suitcase	plane	station

E Listen and sing. Then watch and sing.

Let's Go on a Journey

Let's go on a journey around the world
By land or sea or air.
I want to see different countries,
And make new friends everywhere.

I want to see the country
from a bus,
And walk by a lake and climb a tree.
I want to look at mountains
from a plane.
Do you like the idea? Come with me!

I want to see an island
from a sandy beach,
And go on a boat on the sea.
I have my passport, ticket,
and suitcase.
What an idea! Come with me!

🇺🇸	🇬🇧
country	countryside

Explore Language

A Listen and read. Who is the family visiting?

1

Nathan: That was a long journey.
Elena: Where's the hotel, Dad?
Rolf: Oh, we aren't going to stay in a hotel.
Elena: Really?
Rolf: We're going to stay somewhere better than a hotel. First, we're going to go by bus to the lake. And from the lake, we're going to travel by boat.
Nathan: That's a lot of traveling!
Rolf: And after the boat …
Elena: Yes?
Rolf: You're going to look for Grandma.
Nathan: Grandma?
Rolf: And Grandma's going to take us to her new house.
Nathan and Elena: Hooray!

B Look at A. Complete.

Going to

Grandma	's	going ______	______ us.
We	______		stay in a hotel.

We're going to travel on a boat.
not ~~We're going travel on a boat.~~

Watch Out

C Think and discuss. Then choose.

1 We use *going to* + infinitive to talk about plans in the present / future.

D Listen and say.

E Put the words in order.

1 plane tickets. / going to / Dad's / buy / the

Dad's going to buy the plane tickets.

2 isn't / drive / us. / Aunt Jane / going to

____

3 your / going / You're / need / to / passport.

____

4 going / to / sleep / on the journey. / I'm

____

5 going / eat / to / aren't / at the airport. / We

____

F Play a chain game. Then write.

I'm going to go on a journey.

He's going on a journey and I'm going to swim in the ocean.

I'm going to go on a journey, Zaid's going to swim in the ocean, and ...

How does weather change journeys to school around the world?

A Listen to Daan talk to his dad about his journey to school. How is Daan going to travel there?

snow ☐

rain ☐

rainbow ☐

thunder ☐

lightning ☐

storm ☐

sunny 1

foggy ☐

cloudy ☐

windy ☐

B Listen, say, and number the pictures in **A**.

C What do you think the weather is like now around the world? Make a list. Tell your friend.

D Now listen to Dakila and María. Write the country. Who lives on the side of a valley?

The Philippines   Colombia

a

Dakila ______

b

María ______

E Listen again. Check (✔).

1	Where does Dakila live?	◯ the city	✔ the country
2	What's the weather like when Dakila walks to school?	◯ sunny	◯ cold
3	How long is his journey to school?	◯ one hour	◯ two hours
4	What's María's journey to school like?	◯ fun	◯ boring
5	How does María go to school?	◯ bus	◯ zip line

Is your journey to school the same or different? How can the weather change it?

Explore Language

A Listen and read. Where's Grandma's house?

B Look at A. Complete.

Prepositions of Movement

	through	the forest		______	the mountain
	______	that bridge		under	the bridge
	______	the steps		down	the steps

Look

Always write the preposition after the verb.

C Think and discuss. Then choose.

1 We use prepositions of movement / place to talk about which direction we're going.

D Listen and say.

E Look and complete.

To find the treasure,
go 1 through the forest.

There is a river. Go 2 ______ the bridge,

and then go 3 ______ the mountain and

4 ______ the steps.

The treasure is 5 ______ the waterfall.

F Play *Find the Treasure*. Give directions.

Start at the castle and go around the mountain.

A Watch and listen. Where do Rob and Greta want to travel?

B Watch again. Number the phrases.

Conversation 1

a ☐ I'd like a ticket to Rain Town, please.

b ☐ One-way, please.

c ☐ Would you like a one-way ticket or a round-trip?

d [1] How can I help you?

Conversation 2

e ☐ What day would you like to travel?

f ☐ On Wednesday

g ☐ Here you go.

h [1] I'd like a round-trip ticket to Sun City for next week, please.

round-trip (US) | return (UK)

Pronunciation /r/ and /w/

Listen and say.

rain round sorry would one Wednesday

What other words do you know with these sounds?

C Plan. Think about your trip. Choose (✓) and write.

Transportation: ◯ train ◯ bus ◯ boat ◯ plane

Place: ____________________

When: ◯ today ◯ next week →

Ticket: ◯ one-way ◯ round-trip

Day: ____________________

Time: ◯ morning ◯ afternoon ◯ evening

D Prepare your conversation. Use your ideas from **C** and phrases from **B**.

A **Ticket seller**

How can I help you?

____

____

Have a nice trip!

B **Customer**

____

____

____

Thank you!

E Practice with a friend.

Reflect
Did we say *please*?
Yes / No

Write About It

A Read the email. Who is it to? What's the subject of the email? Circle.

To: harry@globalstage.com
Subject: My Amazing Journey

Hi Harry,

How are you? I'm staying in a hotel in a rainforest. The journey was amazing! We walked to our hotel because you can't drive in a rainforest. First, we walked to the river and over a long bridge. I didn't like it because the river was big. Then, we walked *around a lake, through the forest, and up a mountain.*
Tomorrow we're going to see some animals. I want to see a crocodile!
Write soon,
Isabel

B Look at **A**. Complete.

1 To : harry@globalstage.com

2 ______________ : My Amazing Journey

3 ______________ Harry, How are you?

4 ______________ , Isabel

C Plan. Think about an amazing journey. Complete.

Place
____

Transportation
______________ → ______________
______________ → ______________

Route

The journey was
____

Tomorrow
____

Reflect
Did I use email phrases?

D Write an Amazing Journey email.

Read the questions and draw or write your answers.

What did I do?

What did I learn?

What was my favorite part?

How well did I do?

What can I do next?

- Sing
- Practice
- Talk
- Find out more

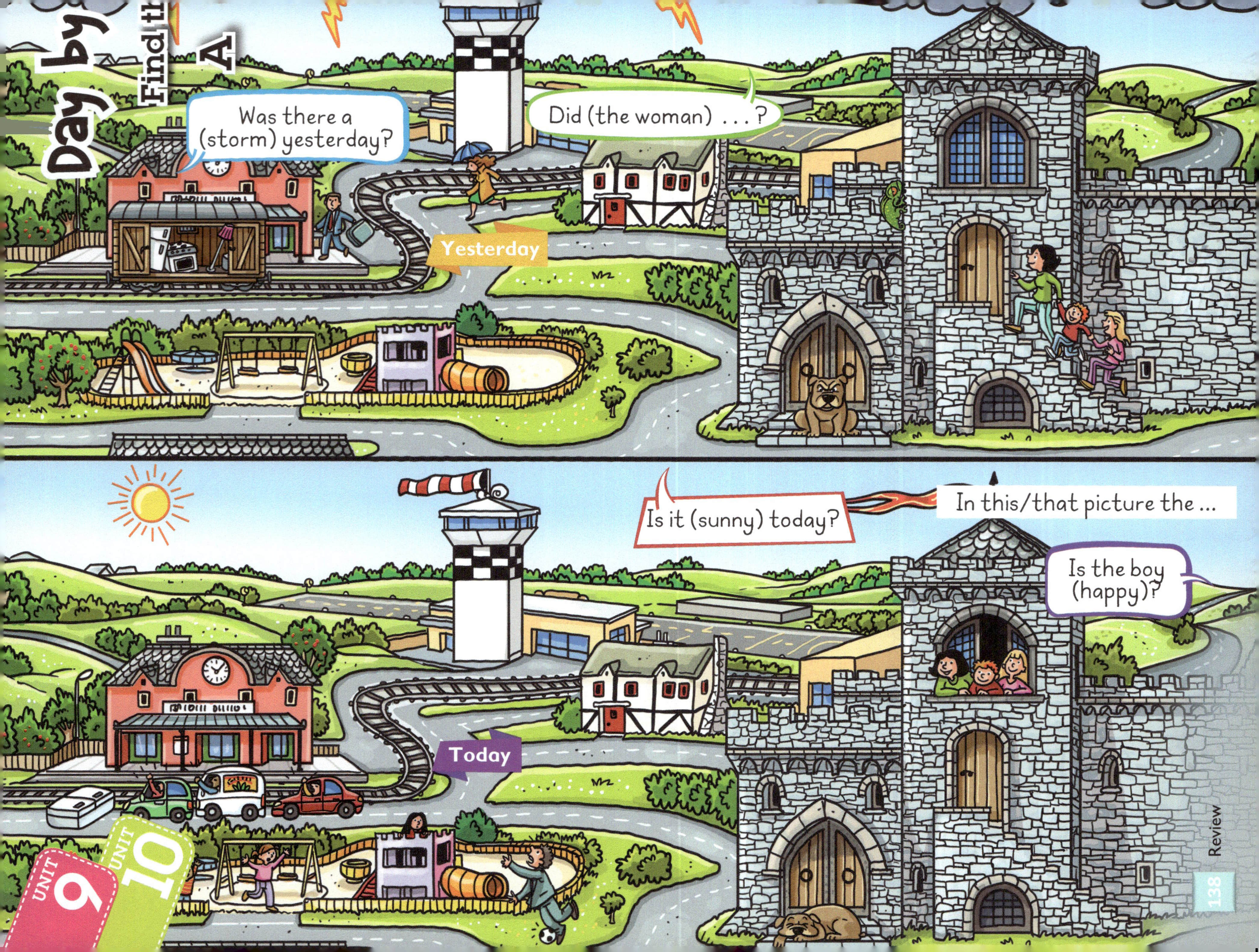
UNIT 9
UNIT 10
Day by
Find th
A
Was there a (storm) yesterday?
Did (the woman) . . . ?
Yesterday
Is it (sunny) today?
In this/that picture the ...
Is the boy (happy)?
Today

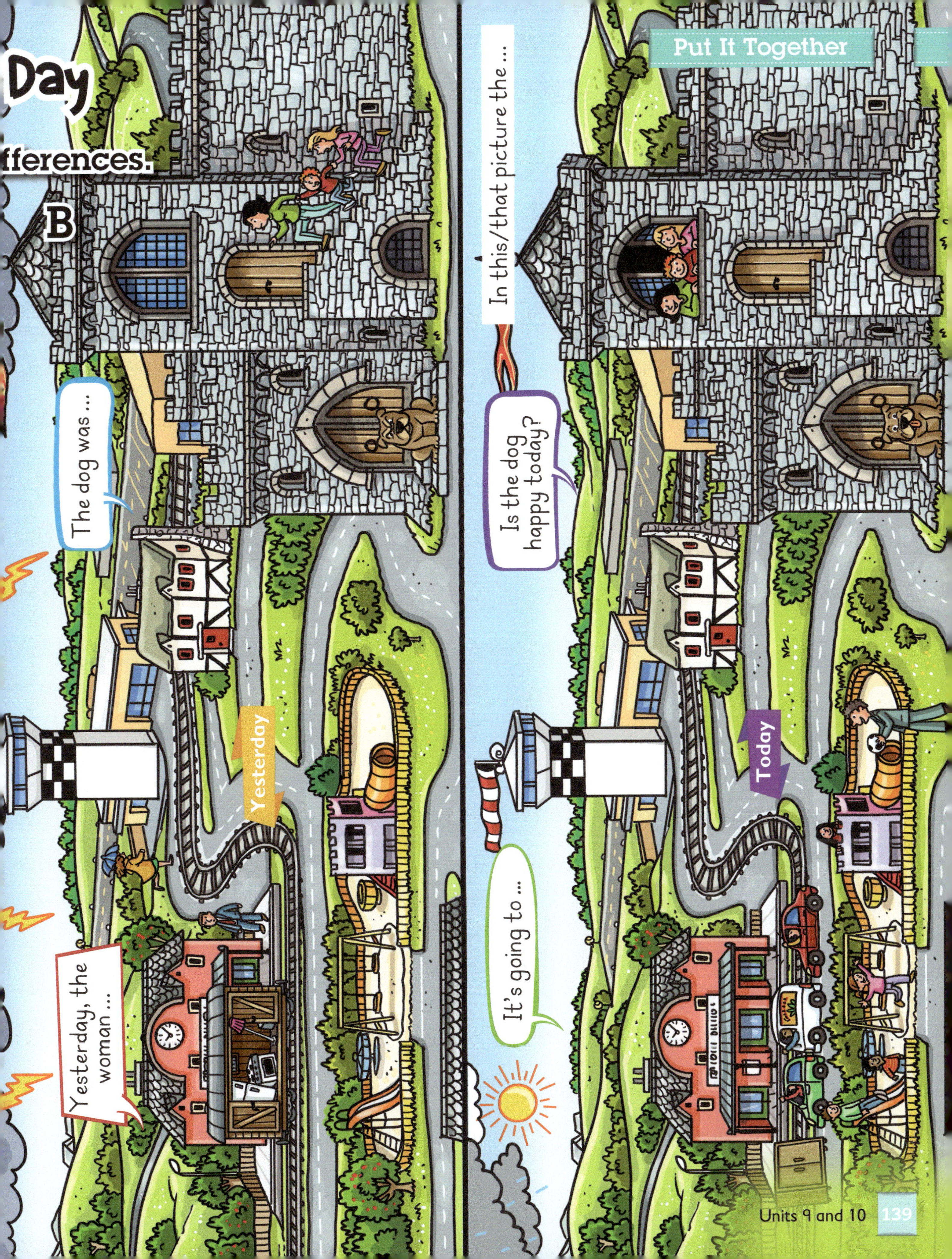
Day
fferences.
B
Yesterday, the woman ...
The dog was ...
Yesterday
It's going to ...
Is the dog happy today?
In this/that picture the ...
Today

Play

Adventures on Purple Mountain

CHARACTERS

Narrator	Rafa
Sean	Mario
Resham	Mom
Ellie	

Narrator: Sean is using his laptop.
Resham: Hi, Sean.What are you doing?
Sean: Hello, Resham and Ellie. I'm *reading about* Purple Mountain. It's *really* beautiful!
Ellie: Let's go there today!
Sean: Great idea, Ellie!

Mom enters.

Sean: Mom! We want to go to Purple Mountain. Is that OK?
Mom: OK. But take my cell phone with you.
Sean: Thanks! Let's tell Mario and Rafa.

Sean, Resham, Ellie, Rafa, and Mario go to Purple Mountain.

Narrator: The friends arrived at Purple Mountain.
Sean: Everybody ready?
All: Yes!
Sean: Let's go!

Chorus: We're walking up the mountain.
Up, up we go …

Rafa: You're walking very slowly. Come on, Mario!

Mario's eating.

Ellie: What are you eating?
Mario: A cupcake.
All: A cupcake?
Mario: I didn't have my breakfast! I'm hungry!
Sean: Come on!

Mario's still eating.

Ellie: What are you eating now, Mario?
Mario: Some potato chips.
Rafa: How much food do you have?
Mario: A bag of potato chips, a box of cookies, and a bag of cherries. And, I had a cupcake.

Resham: You're very hungry!
Sean: Look down there! There's a lake.
Ellie: And look at the river. You can see it go all the way to the ocean!
Rafa: This is a great place!
Sean: Let's go.

Chorus: We're walking up the mountain.
Up, up we go.
You're walking very slowly.
Come on, Mario!

Resham: Oh, look! There's a forest.

Sean, Resham, Ellie, and Rafa go into the forest.

Narrator: The friends were lost in the forest!
Rafa: Where are we?
Sean: This is a little scary!
Resham: Call your mom!
Sean: The cell phone isn't working!
Ellie: Listen! Can you hear that noise in the trees?
Resham: What is it?
Rafa: Is it a dangerous animal?
Sean: Is it a bear?
Ellie: It's coming! Oh, no!

Mario appears.

Mario: Hi, everyone!
Resham: It's you, Mario!
Mario: What's the matter?
Sean: We don't know where we are!
Ellie: And we can't get home.
Mario: Yes, we can. Look!
Rafa: We can follow your food crumbs!
Resham: Great, Mario!

Chorus: We're walking down the mountain.
Down, down we go.
We're following the crumbs!
Thank you, Mario!

King Grandpa's Treasure

CHARACTERS

Narrator	Princess Mom
King Grandpa	Young Prince Eric
Queen Grandma	Sofia, Eric's friend
Prince Dad	Ramón, Eric's friend

Narrator: It was summer. Sofia and Ramón went to Eric's castle on vacation, but Eric's family wasn't happy.
Eric: Hi. *Can you help us?*
Sofia: Yes. What's the matter?
King Grandpa: It's my treasure.
Queen Grandma: We don't know where it is.
Ramón: We can look for it.
Prince Dad: Yes, but our castle has a lot of rooms!
Eric: Let's work in teams. We can look in different rooms.
Princess Mom: That's a *great idea*! Let's go.

Chorus: We're looking for the treasure
And we're working together!

Narrator: King Grandpa and Prince Dad went down to the basement.
Prince Dad: It's messy. I'm scared.
King Grandpa: Me, too!
Prince Dad: I'm going to look in the cabinets.

Prince Dad opens the door.

King Grandpa: Did you find my treasure?
Prince Dad: No, I didn't. Sorry, but I found my boat.
King Grandpa: Ooh!

Chorus: We're looking for the treasure
And we're working together!

Narrator: Queen Grandma and Princess Mom climbed the tower.
Queen Grandma: This was my playroom. I played here with my cousins.
Princess Mom: I can't see the treasure here. What's that small building?
Queen Grandma: It's a model castle. I built it for your birthday.
Princess Mom: Thank you! It's wonderful.

Chorus: We're looking for the treasure
And we're working together!

Narrator: Eric, Ramón, and Sofia went to the king's bedroom.

Eric: This is the biggest bedroom in the castle.
Sofia: These paintings are beautiful.
Eric: This is the most famous painting.
Narrator: Ramón touched the painting. It opened, and there was a secret room.
Ramón: Oops. Sorry!
Eric: This is exciting!
Sofia: Come on!

They go inside.

Ramón: What's this big box?
Eric: That's King Grandpa's treasure.
Sofia: Hooray! Can you help me carry it?
Ramón: Yes, we can.

Chorus: We're looking for the treasure
And we're working together!

Narrator: Eric, Sofia, and Ramón carried the treasure into the Great Hall.
Ramón: We found your treasure!
Eric: It was in a secret room.
All: Great job!
King Grandpa: Thank you so much.
Sofia: What's the treasure?
King Grandpa: Look!

King Grandpa opens the treasure box.

King Grandpa: These are my favorite things.
All: Oooohhhh!
Ramón: Why is that treasure?
Queen Grandma: Because they're the most important things from his life.
King Grandpa: I traveled on this plane! And I ran in this race!
Prince Dad: It's like my boat!
Princess Mom: And my model castle!

They hear the clock ring.

Eric: It's 2 o'clock.
Princess Mom: Let's eat lunch.
King Grandpa: And after, I'm going to tell you about my trips!
All: With your treasure!

Chorus: We have the treasure
And we're working together!

Macmillan Education
4 Crinan Street
London N1 9XW
A division of Springer Nature Limited

Companies and representatives throughout the world

Language Book ISBN 978-1-786-32349-1
Student Book Pack 978-1-380-00224-2

Text, design and illustration © Springer Nature Limited 2019
Written by Roisin O'Farrell and Jeanette Corbett
Additional material written by Michelle Worgan, Viv Lambert, and Mo Choy

The authors have asserted their right to be identified as the authors of this work in accordance with the Copyright, Designs and Patents Act 1988.

First published 2019

All rights reserved. No part of this publication may be reproduced, stored in a retrieval system, or transmitted in any form or by any means, electronic, mechanical, photocopying, recording, or otherwise, without the prior written permission of the publishers.

Original design by D'Sign Lab and EMC Design Ltd.
Page make-up by D'Sign Lab
Illustrated by Beatrice Bencivioni (Beehive): 100–103, 106, 110–113; D'Sign Lab: 21, 33, 47, 65, 72, 73, 85, 98–99, 111, 125, 137; Donald Wo (MB Artists): 22–25, 28–29, 32, 34–35; Luispa (Lemonade): 114–118, 120–121, 124–125; Gustavo Mazali (Lemonade): 88–91, 94, 99; Moreno Chiachiera (Lemonade): 126–129, 132–133, 138–139; Emiliano Ordás: 6–12, 16, 18–19, 21, 30–31, 36–39, 42–51, 54–64, 68, 70–71, 73, 82–83, 96–97, 108–109, 122–123, 134–135, 140–143; Jomike Tejido (MB Artists): 74–77, 80, 84–87.
Cover design and concept by 3CD
Cover adaptation by Roberto Martinez
Cover photos by Getty Images/Iconica/Flashpop (boy), Getty Images/Leonello Calvetti/Stocktrek Images (globe)
Cover photos retouched by Hal Silverman Studio
Picture research by Penelope Bowden (Proudfoot Pictures)

Authors' acknowledgements
We would like to thank everyone at Macmillan and RedNova Learning for their encouragement and direction in bringing this book to life. We are also very grateful to our work colleagues and students for their contributions and inspiration, especially the teachers and students of ELI, Sevilla and Academia Británica, Huelva. Finally, we would like to thank our families and friends for their motivational support: Freddy, George, Sofía, Ramón and Ana for sharing their child-like perspective, and Nuala, Els, Harriet, Brendan and Ramón for their patience and understanding.

The publishers would like to thank: Salwa Abid, Meryem Bennis, Leticia Blázquez, Angel Bonilla, Victor Cojulun, John Cruft, Silvia Díez de Rivera, Randa Farouk, Magda Giomazi, Vangelina Hernández, Quyen Ho, Ziad Jadallah, Youngkwang Jang, Faisal M'reish, Riham Almughrabi, Jackie Mustoe, Adriana Ochoa, Devrim Ozdemir, Maria Pia Ayala, Silvia Raya, Ola Refaat, Helen Sharbain, Sana Sifri, Esra Tosun, Lemmy Trujillo, Tamer Victor, Jake Whiddon, Sandra Wu, Amanda Zhang, Colegio Buckingham and Gabriela Rodríguez, Colegio Euterpe and Angélica Sánchez, Colegio Héroes Mexicanos and Marcelo Carlos Hernández Morales, Internaciones Campus Fraijanes and Ana Monica Thomas, New Victoria International College and Ghada Hassan Mokbel, The Southern Cross School and Dayana Acevedo, Antonia Lira, and Paula Jorquera, Verbo Quetzaltenango and Cindy Steicy Ixchiu Velásquez

The authors and publishers would like to thank the following for permission to reproduce their photographs: **Alamy**/age fotostock p119(l), Alamy/Ian Allenden pp14(cl), 93(r), Alamy/Richard Codington p41(l), Alamy/Li Ding p26(bcr), Alamy/Hero Images Inc p14(main), Alamy/Artem Konovalov p78(bcm), Alamy/Erich Kuchling/Westend61 GmbH p40(main), Alamy/Craig Lovell p136, Alamy/lovethephoto p14(tl), Alamy/Maria Meester p130(bcr), Alamy/Pegaz p67(r), Alamy/Peter Schatz/Powerpics p130(br), Alamy/Chris Rout p26(c), Alamy/Valentyn Volkov p27(r); **Digital Vision** p40(tcr); **FLPA**/Frans Lanting p40(bm), FLPA/Thorsten Negro, Imagebroker p40(tm), FLPA/Filippo Nucifora/Minden Pictures p40(br), FLPA/Photo Researchers p40(tr); **Getty Images**/Ableimages p92(c), Getty Images/Alistair Berg p52(bcr), Getty Images/Blend Images – KidStock pp52(bm), 104(br), Getty Images/BLOOM image p78(bm), Getty Images/romana chapman p93(l), Getty Images/DeepDesertPhoto p130(cm), Getty Images/deeepblue p26(tm), Getty Images/Kevin Dodge p104(c), Getty Images/Steven Errico p14(bcr), Getty Images/EujarimPhotography p52(cl), Getty Images/FatCamera p52(tm), Getty Images/FlairImages p92(tm), Getty Images/Priscilla Gragg p52(tcr), Getty Images/grandriver p15(l), Getty Images/Jamie Grill p52(br), Getty Images/Jamie Grill/Blend Images – JGI p14(tm), Getty Images/Philippe Henry p66(tcr), Getty Images/Hero Images pp52(c), 92(main, br), Getty Images/Nicole Hill/Rubberball p104(cl), Getty Images/Andrew Holt p66(tr), Getty Images/Imgorthand p131(r), Getty Images/Indeed p53(l), Getty Images/Jupiterimages p14(tcr), Getty Images/Nadeem Khawar p67(l), Getty Images/Sungjin Kim p119(r), Getty Images/Fabrice LEROUGE p78(tl), Getty Images/Randi Linford/EyeEm p66(bcl), Getty Images/LittleBee80 p92(tl), Getty Images/loops7 p130(tl), Getty Images/Tim Martin p130(tcr), Getty Images/Graham Monro/gm photographics p40(bl), Getty Images/Hans Neleman p53(r), Getty Images/Liam Norris/Cultura RM Exclusive p92(tr), Getty Images/Seb Oliver/Cultura p118, Getty Images/James Porter p15(r), Getty Images/Franz Pritz p104(bcr), Getty Images/Radius Images p130(bc), Getty Images/Grady Reese/Corbis/VCG p104(tr), Getty Images/Christopher Robbins p130(main), Getty Images/silversaltphoto.j.senosiain p41(r), Getty Images/simonkr p105(l), Getty Images/simonlong p27(l), Getty Images/SolStock p14(br), Getty Images/Paul A. Souders p130(cl), Getty Images/Rudy Sulgan p78(main), Getty Images/Tejal_pandya p66(c), Getty Images/Leanne Temme p52(tr), Getty Images/travellinglight p26(br), Getty Images/Thinkstock Images p78(tcr), Getty Images/ULTRA.F p104(bm), Getty Images/urbancow p104(tcr), Getty Images/Vstock LLC/Tetra Images p66(br), Getty Images/wakila p66(bm), Getty Images/Simon Watson p52(tl), Getty Images/ziggy_mars p131(l); **Glow Images**/Hermann Dobler p79(l), Glow Images/Hero/Corbis p66(main); **Nature Picture Library**/John Cancalosi p66(bcr); plainpicture/Lars-Olof Johansson/Johner p130(tr), **plainpicture**/Chris Ryan/Caiaimages p130(tm); **Shutterstock**/Africa Studio p26(tr), Shutterstock/Borja Andreu p78(tm), Shutterstock/Pitak Areekul p78(tc), Shutterstock/Davizro Photography p78(tr), Shutterstock/ESB Professional p52(main), Shutterstock/Jack Frog p104(main), Shutterstock/Keep Smiling Photography p105(r), Shutterstock/Yuganov Konstantin p92(tcr), Shutterstock/luanateutzi p78(bcr, br), Shutterstock/Maxim Lysenko p79(r), Shutterstock/Kelly Marken p66(bl), Shutterstock/Nagel Photography p40(bcr), Shutterstock/nikkytok p14(tr), Shutterstock/Tyler Olson p92(tcl), Shutterstock/Tarr Pichet p26(tl), Shutterstock/racom p104(bl), Shutterstock/Ljupco Smokovski p26(main), Shutterstock/Parinya Suwannagood p26(tcr)

These materials may contain links for third party websites. We have no control over, and are not responsible for, the contents of such third party websites. Please use care when accessing them.

The inclusion of any specific companies, commercial products, trade names or otherwise, does not constitute or imply its endorsement or recommendation by Springer Nature Limited.

Printed and bound in Uruguay

2023

3 5